HIDING BEHIND A WINDOW

MY STORY OF STEPPING OUT FROM BEHIND A WINDOW, MOVING FORWARD AFTER TRAUMA, AND RECLAIMING WHAT WAS LOST

LAURA CHILL

author HOUSE®

AuthorHouse™
1663 Liberty Drive
Bloomington, IN 47403
www.authorhouse.com
Phone: 833-262-8899

Published by AuthorHouse 05/27/2021

ISBN: 978-1-6655-2755-2 (sc)
ISBN: 978-1-6655-2753-8 (hc)
ISBN: 978-1-6655-2754-5 (e)

Library of Congress Control Number: 2021910876

Print information available on the last page.

Any people depicted in stock imagery provided by Getty Images are models, and such images are being used for illustrative purposes only. Certain stock imagery © Getty Images.

This book is printed on acid-free paper.

To my mom and dad:
Your unconditional love and support filled my
heart, making me the women I am.
To my babies:
my warmhearted son and daughter, you always helped
make moving forward so much easier.
I love you both more than words can say!

Thank you to my friends, you know who you are, for listening to me cry and dump, and process while completing this book. I want to thank my husband for standing by my side as I maneuver these events through my head.

Thank you to all the therapist, psychiatrist, clinicians, and nurses that have listened to all the hard stuff. Your tools are not just stored away collecting dust.

A special thank you to the one therapist that never left me feeling dismissed. I was encouraged to step out from behind the window, without judgement, and with praise for every step I took moving forward.

Last but not least, thank you to my research assistant for helping to put pieces of the puzzle together with me.

I'm blessed; a huge thank you to you all!

AUTHOR'S NOTE

Thank you, reader, for giving me this opportunity to share this journey full of unfortunate events and beautiful moments.

'Moving forward' stuck as a personal mantra after having two different cars that did not work in reverse. I would use my left leg to push myself out of parking spaces or parked in places where I could use gravity to roll backwards. Shortly after one of these cars left me stranded on the roadside for the last time, I went to a car lot and for the first time, chose my own vehicle. In this moment of independence, I reminded myself that I was in charge of moving myself forward.

DISCLAIMER

The names of friends have been changed to protect privacy. The names of abusers have been removed from this story to protect the author. Many event involving drug use and sexual activity have been left out, despite the author's desire to provide full transparency. All content contained within this book is from my memories and my perspective of reality throughout my life. It has never been my intention to hurt others with my story. It has, however, provided me the opportunity to make sense of the hard things and to help me heal.

PREFACE

"The study of psychological trauma has an 'underground' history. Like traumatized people, we have been cut off from the knowledge of our past. Like traumatized people, we need to understand the past in order to reclaim the present and future. Therefore, an understanding of psychological trauma begins with rediscovering history."[1]

I'm standing behind a window, watching everyone else on the other side. I jump and wave my hands at them, willing them to look through the glass and see me there. Some walk past without a pause. Could they not see me? Others stop briefly, their gazes caught by my frantic gestures, only to turn away. They pretend not to see, quickly walking past. Maybe they did not recognize my actions as cries for help. I will never know what they thought as they saw me there— observed and unseen.

How can it be possible to hide behind windows?

How can we be clearly visible yet completely overlooked?

This story can be hard for some, eye-opening for others, and triggering for far too many. For me, telling this story is therapeutic. By telling my story, I take back some of that which was taken from me. Until recently, I would have preferred to think about these memories as if they belonged to someone else—another little girl who was not me. Or maybe that these events happened to many children, all different ages with different names and faces. I wanted these memories to belong to anyone but me. I wanted

---

[1] Judith Lewis Herman, *Trauma and Recovery* (New York, NY: Basic Books, 2015), 2.

to disown them, dismiss them, and forget them all together. I didn't want to acknowledge how they had shaped me or how they had influenced so much of my life.

Why did I write about the unfortunate events I experienced? Why revisit traumatic memories so hard-fought to be forgotten? Therapy has taught me that to keep moving forward, we must address that which holds us in the past. It is necessary to understand what was lost in the past in order to reclaim it for the present and future. I want to reclaim what was lost. So, I continue to move forward. Telling this story has helped me do that. I believe this is the only positive way to go on day-to-day while consequences happen, and hard lessons are learned. I'll just keep moving forward.

Although my story is marked by trauma, I want to express that my childhood was not unhappy. There were many beautiful moments that I treasure. There was much love in my family, many joyful memories. I know that my parents loved me unconditionally. They provided me with the best care they knew how to provide, and I will always be grateful to them.

1

FAMILY

"As we grow up, we gradually learn to take care of ourselves, both physically and emotionally, but we get our first lessons in self-care from the way we are cared for. Children whose parents are reliable sources of comfort and strength have a lifetime advantage—a kind of buffer against the worst that fate can hand them."[2]

My parents tried for ten years to have their first child together—me. My momma says I was born with dark fuzzy fur on my neck, shoulders, back, and ears. She would say that I looked like a baby monkey. Starting as an infant, I was called more by my nickname than my legal name. I'm not sure why this started, but my nickname has stuck with me to this day. A short drop from a babysitter's arms resulted in a broken collarbone before my first birthday. This injury didn't slow down my development too much, and according to my baby book, I was walking at nine months. I can imagine mom holding my little hands for support as I practiced putting one foot in front of the other, just as I have done with my own children and many that I have cared for throughout my life. When I started to speak, my parents delighted in my baby speak: elephants became '*elefunks*,' lady bugs were '*lady-bucks*,' and boys and girls were '*boys and gwees*.' Even as an adult, I still loved it when my dad called me his '*gwee*.'

As I can imagine their joy at my progress, I can just as easily imagine

---

[2] Bessel Van der Kolk, *The Body Keeps the Score: Brain, Mind, and Body in the Healing of Trauma* (New York, NY: Penguin Books, 2015), 112.

their shock at my less-than-adorable behaviors. One of my favorite tricks to pull as a baby was to remove my poopy diaper and use it to finger-paint in my crib or whatever part of the wall I could reach. By the time I was three or four, I would store food in my cheeks like a chipmunk for quite a while after meals. My relationship with food has never been great. Its smell, texture, or the look of it was rarely pleasing to me and my mom said that I didn't like to eat very much, even then. An exception to this distaste for eating, around the time I was in preschool, was my favorite snack that I loved hunting for—the banana slugs found in my home state, Washington. *Nummy!*

When driving into our little town, you would pass by this quaint wood and stone building. That was my preschool. I have fun memories of being up on a big stage, which was the dramatic play area. I remember it being huge as a four-year old. On the other side of the large, open space of the school, I remember there being a sand or sensory table. I have fond memories of kindergarten too. I remember liking sitting in a carpeted area, presumably a library and quiet play area that was away from our desks. Despite all the negative experiences that came after this time, I'm still grateful that at this point in my life, I was loved and nurtured by the adults around me.

I am from a small town in the Pacific Northwest. My momma was involved at our school and the PTA. She attended and hosted church events, volunteering hundreds of hours of her time. She even worked at local strawberry farms for a few summers when I young. When I was in second grade, she opened and ran an in-home childcare program. When I was sixteen years old, I was old enough to go with her to Child and Adult CPR and First Aid trainings. I also started accompanying her to early childcare conferences. We would attend trainings in huge conference rooms in Seattle. In between the speakers, we would walk to all the various tables and booths that showcased arts and crafts' materials, preschool programs, toys, clothing, and anything else you could imagine in relation to early childcare. What I did not know then was that what started with shadowing my mom ended up being a thirty-five-year long career, before my own retirement from the early childcare field.

As much as my mother loved my little brother, me, and all her daycare babies, she also loved her alone time. As an adult who also decided to run a childcare program, I can deeply understand and appreciate this. Mom enjoyed playing pinochle and loved her bingo. She would close her childcare business a half an hour early on bingo nights to be in the doorway, ready to leave at 5:30 pm, with her purse and bingo bag in hand, as soon as that last kiddo left. Years later, after my brother and I had left the house, she was extremely proud of getting herself a cute little two-seater car. Mom would say that this car was for her and her bingo bag—there was no room for anyone else!

I can't even begin to say enough about my momma to fully explain what an amazing, funny, unconditionally loving, compassionate, and beautiful person she was. I remember laughing with her so hard until food would fly out our mouths—sometimes we even peed. We went with mom most summers to her mother's, our grandma. Her house was always pretty quiet and perfectly kept. For one of our visits, I brought my elementary school best friend. I remember the three of us lying on the bed in the spare room—it was so quiet! It was so quiet that the smallest noise gave us all the giggles. Tears were coming out of my eyes I was laughing so hard, and then lost control my bladder. I remember mom laughing, changing the sheets, and shushing us to quiet snickers.

Going to grandma's meant going to Oregon and visiting the ocean. We would drive up Oregon's coast, on our way to the water where we would run in the waves, play in the sand, and find gorgeous agates, or whatever else we could find in the surf. The evenings provided breath-taking views of the sun setting over the water. I still think of mom whenever I see the sky cast in gorgeous sunset or sunrise colors. The drive was always nice too. When we got close to the state border, which we crossed going over the Washington/Oregon bridge, mom would always put her foot as far forward on the floor as she could, then inform us that made it to Oregon first. I always thought that joke was funny. We would revisit this route for family reunions in Oregon for family reunions in the summer. There is a Chinese restaurant in the area where mom and I would stop in. My favorite memory of our spot will always be the time mom and I sat there over a cup of tea and laughed so hard that we were crying and trying not to pee. I could truly write a whole other book on just the things I did with mom.

After she passed away, I remember thinking about our trip to this restaurant and how I didn't know at the time that it would be our last time visiting our spot. This trip took place shortly after mom had become very sick from the effects of chemotherapy. Some may find talking about one's own death morbid, but she was not one of those people. We discussed how she would always be with me, even going as far as to discuss how she would communicate her presence. She said that she would try to get my attention by flashing lights. I agreed to her plan but lightheartedly asked her to please not scare the daylights out of me by doing that. This conversation was not very serious, but I still think of her when the lights flicker or go out unexpectedly. She is missed by me every day.

My daddy worked in Alaska on the pipelines when I was an infant. He came home to have a few sales jobs, than became a union laborer. He later accomplished his goal of starting his own construction company. Daddy spent a lot of the time fishing and being outdoors. He appreciated making his own moonshine. He loved his shine and was happy to share the distillation process with his kids, teaching us the science behind the shine once we were old enough to learn it. He was always proud to share the results with friends and family.

Dad was adventurous. He loved racing motorcycles and chose my birthday and first initial for his racing number. In his younger years, he also enjoyed the sport of boxing. He even went on to coach a boxing champion. I remember my glee of having a real-life speed bag in our basement when I was a kid. I thought that was so fun.

Dad was an artist, full of the artistic talent that seems to run in our family. For years in our town, you could drive around and see the signs he designed, painted, and constructed for local businesses. I still hold on to the *Day Care* sign that he made for mom's childcare program. He painted a picture of 2 cartoon characters, swinging on swings. He also named his asphalt business *the "Same as the Day Care"*

Our dad was always the biggest supporter of us kids. He was always letting us know that we could do anything we set our minds to and work hard at. Our deep discussions are missed, his unconditional acceptance is missed, and even his orneriness is missed. Dad was eventually diagnosed with cancer and ended up having to have part of his voice box removed. This meant that he could no longer yell. If you were a worker on a jobsite with him, you might have low-key appreciated this. After his surgery, he had a low, rough voice. You would be surprised, however, how well he could get your attention with a whistle or a look. He never lost his strength of will to live how he wanted. When he first came out of surgery, he had a tract in his throat that he quickly learned to blow smoke out of. Even though it seemed to pain him whenever he talked, he continued to delight in sharing stories with all who would listen. My dad was truly at home in our community. Whether it was pig roasts, local gatherings, or musical events, my dad and our family were surrounded by friends and the people who knew us. I always felt so proud about how loved he was by so many.

I have two brothers. One is three years younger than me and the other is ten years older. My older sibling is my half-brother from my daddy's first marriage, and I'm as proud of him as my brother as anyone could be. Both of my siblings have special places in my heart.

Some of my favorite memories of my family together were the times we would all float down the Snoqualmie River together. Every summer since I can remember, my family would get in dad's drift boat and float down the River. Mom and I would always sit toward the front of the boat, snacking and sunbathing. Occasionally, my mom, little brother, and I would float the river on inner-tubes with dad's boat floating somewhere near behind us. It was extra fun when my older brother and his friends, or even my dad's friends, would float with us too. It was always an exciting event when a couple dozen tubes and river boats floated down the river together. This mass of floaters was sometimes referred to as the Local Yacht Club.'

When I was very young, I remember pulling off to the side of the riverbank and playing with the natural gray clay that lines part of the river dyke. There was also a rope swing with a little beachy area partway down the float. I never used the rope swing, but I enjoyed watching my older brother and his friends launch themselves into the water using it. A bit further down, right before the slow part of the river, was a golf course off to one side. I doubt we were the only ones who returned from floating with golf balls fetched from the bottom of the river. The most fun part of the float was going over the rapids, of course. That part was always exciting.

Spending time near rivers is still one of my favorite places to escape and unwind. I enjoy listening to the water and trying to capture the beauty of the water hitting the rocks in my sketches. The river and its sounds always take me back to my memories of having fun playing with the other kids in and around the water. I find river sounds so soothing that it has become my go-to background noise for meditation. Behind the house where I raised my kids, there is a good-sized creek that had some simple bridges made from fallen logs, connecting the two banks in various places along the hiking trails that followed the water's path. I absolutely loved sitting near the creek on the nearest log and getting lost in a good book. Other times I would sketch what caught my eye that day or just pray or talk to mom in heaven. Being near and listening to the water always brought the same sense of calm. After moving to Oregon, I was able to find a couple of new favorite river spots. I don't visit the river as often as I used to, but it the sense of emotional and physical freedom is always enjoyed when I do.

2

INNOCENCE TAKEN

> "Traumatic memories have a number of unusual qualities. They are not encoded like the ordinary memories of adults in a verbal, linear narrative that is assimilated into an ongoing life story. Traumatic memories lack verbal narrative and context; rather, they are encoded in the form of vivid sensations and images."[3]

Like many five-year old children, I was a friendly and curious kid. I was always eager to demonstrate to the adults in my life that I was capable like a 'big person.' One day, my friend and neighbor, a little girl close to me in age, and I went to visit a different neighbor who lived down the street. In his early years, this man worked at and owned a local mill. For this story, I will refer to him as Abuser A. His wife had died recently, and the old man now lived alone in his home. My friend and I were proud to be out visiting neighbors on our own. I remember feeling very tall and proud as we excitedly walked to his house that day. The sun was bright, casting light along our path. It was so warm, and my world felt safe.

After we arrived at Abuser A's home, we were invited in. We entered through the glass sliding doors that opened to a kitchen with a wooden table placed at its center. I remember the sorry state of that kitchen. The glass in the sliders was so dirty that you could barely see through it. The wooden table and kitchen counters were covered in clutter and partially consumed food items. I thought that it must have been his wife who had

---

[3] Herman, *Trauma and Recovery*, 37-38

made sure the house was tidy. Her absence was profoundly felt in this ill-kept space.

My friend and I spoke to Abuser A in that kitchen for a few minutes, about what I cannot remember. During this conversation, I was invited to sit in Abuser A's lap. I complied and then conversation continued. After a little while, Abuser A asked if we would like to watch some television. We jumped up excitedly from our seated positions and were led down a narrow, dark hallway that was covered in pictures, into the large front room. As we entered the room, I saw the gigantic brick fireplace and towering bookshelves along the walls. So many books! There were large, cushioned chairs in the middle of the room that faced the fireplace and television. To this day, that fireplace stands, covered in vines and blackberry bushes, towering over the gigantic, mossy rock I was baptized next to. Everything seems so grand when you are that small. I do remember what was *not* grand about this place, however, was its smell. The smell was present throughout the house but got stronger as we walked down that hallway. It was a musty, wet stench. Was it the dirty carpet? Was that just how old people smell? The smell was cloying; sickly sweet, old, and seemed to muffle sound, making this space too quiet to be comfortable.

The television turning on distracted us from the eerie quiet and unpleasant odor. My friend hopped up onto one of the cushioned chairs, already focused on whatever was on the screen. Before I got the chance to choose my own place to sit, Abuser A came up to stand behind me, and told me to keep watching the TV. My arms were gently and quietly held behind me so that my hands touched the bump in his jeans. My mind flooded with confusion. *What's this? What's going on?* My confusion took on an air of fear as I was led away from my friend and the television, into a small bedroom toward the back of the house. I was placed on the edge of the bed, on top of the old comforter. I saw his gray hair and old, fat face leering down at me. I squeezed my eyes shut, wanting it all to go away. Then, on my mouth, closed as tightly as my eyelids, I felt something wet. Then it was touching my lips and face. I opened my eyes briefly to see what was happening. I was shocked when I saw his penis hovering so close to my face. My eyes snapped shut again, recoiling from him. I whimpered as I felt the small hole at the tip of his disgusting old penis continue to touch my face as he tried to force it into my mouth. As my whimpering continued and I resisted, he whispered to me to be quiet and told me not to cry. He kept talking and I kept wishing that I could just go home. I was so scared and just wanted to go home. After it was over, I hazily remember being led back out to where my friend continued to watch tv, innocently unaware of what that bad old man had just done to her friend. Again, I was forced to stand in front of Abuser A, behind the chair my friend sat on, as the television droned on. I was scared, confused, and unsure what I had just experienced. I was acutely aware of his position behind me and so I was quiet, just like he told me to be. It was like some of the silence that filled that house seeped into me.

Seeing my friend in that chair was my last clear memory of her. I assume that we had seen each other a few times after since we were friends and she lived across the street from me, but my family moved homes shortly after that day and we lost touch. As an adult, I have often wondered what had inspired this visit. Were we sent there, or did we decide to do so? How was it deemed safe that two kindergarten-aged children were sent to visit alone with an old widower? Did anything ever happen to my friend like it did to me? I think back to those dirty, cloudy windows through which we entered the home. Those windows hid what was truly disgusting and dirty inside that house.

3

NEW HOME

"Parents should be aware of sudden changes in behavior: nightmares; withdrawal and avoidance of particular persons, places, or things; and unusual aggressiveness, jumpiness, and/or inappropriate sexual behavior."[4]

We moved from our house across from my friend into a large country house on the other side of town. I remember passing by flowers, fields of wildflowers, and pastures where horses lived serenely among brightly speckled natural beauty as we made our way to our new home. The road that led up to that house would become where I first practiced driving, starting by sitting on dad's lap and keeping the wheel straight while he worked the pedals. I'm pretty sure my younger brother had this memorable experience as well. We both now had bunk beds in our new home. Across the hall from our room was our playroom. There were wall-to-wall toys, an easel for painting, and more coloring books than I could ever color. I was delighted by our country home. It was a beautiful, peaceful place to play; we were safe and free to explore. Never mind the hive of bees we discovered living in the brick fireplace, whose long neck stretched up through the ceiling; we just stayed away from that.

Occasionally, momma would bring us to her friend who had a small

---

[4] Judith A. Cohen, Anthony P. Mannarino, and Esther Deblinger, *Treating Trauma and Traumatic Grief in Children and Adolescents*, Second Edition (New York: The Guilford Press, 2017), 306.

daycare in her home. My favorite time was lunchtime when we were served warm tomato soup and crispy, gooey grilled-cheese sandwiches. I remember her friend doing her best to encourage us to take naps. I am not sure if she was ever successful in doing so. My memories of naptime are made up primarily of us laughing, rolling and tumbling around on the large bed, and giggling at our mischief.

My mother did her best to teach us independence and I remember some of those lessons being taught to me in that house. I had officially started kindergarten and took the bus to and from school. Momma told me that if I got off the bus and she was not home to let me inside, that I was to go straight to our new neighbor's house and knock on their door. I learned when I was older that she tested me on this lesson. One day, just before the time my bus would drop me off, she went to across the street to another neighbor's house. From inside, she looked out their front window to see if I would do as she had told me to do. Instead of going over to the neighbors, however, she saw me sit down on our steps and cry. I imagine she saw this emotional display as shyness, as any other child might feel when faced with the prospect of interacting with new people. I don't see how she could have recognized that at this point, I no longer felt safe going over to a neighbor's house alone.

My momma, little brother, and I lived in this big house with its never-ending fields and blossoming crabapple tress for only a little while. At this time, I knew that daddy was away in Alaska, working in the snow on a big important pipeline. We often received letters and I remember momma reading them out loud to us, showing us the pictures that he sent.

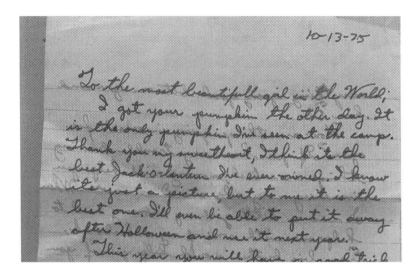

Letter from dad

"To the most beautiful girl in the world; 10-13-1975

I got your pumpkin the other day. It is the only pumpkin I've seen in camp. Thank you my sweetheart, I think it's the best Jack-o-lantern I've owned. I know it's just a picture but to me it's the best one. I'll even be able to put it away for next year.

This year you will have a good "trick or treat" night I hope. You'll even have a party at school again I'll bet. Do you remember how much fun you had at the school carnival last Halloween? Just remember not to take candy from anyone unless your mommy says it's ok. Of course I know you already know that, right?

Are you and brother getting along with each other? I love you both so much that I want to see you forever happy. He is the only little brother you got and I know he loves you a whole bunch too.

How about big-brother; Is everything going good between you and him? How are things going in school? If you have any trouble learning things in school, mommy will help you in every way she can I am sure. When I was a little girl (*He joked like this for as long as I can remember*) my mommy would help me with some of my school work. Even big brother would help you if you asked him.

I sure would like to know what you are going to dress up like for your school Halloween party. I sure wish I was there to help you get dressed and take you around to do your trick-or-treating. Halloween is so much fun because you can be anything or anybody you want to be. Even a scary monster if you want. Have a good time my pretty girl. I'm going to bed now, so I will say goodnight to you in this letter and good night to your picture hanging on my wall. I love you more than anybody in the world,

Daddy"

When I was about six, daddy came home from Alaska and we moved out of our big house in the fields. Our family was growing, and we needed more space. The new house was old with big rooms, like the country house, but had just one story. What the new house did have, that the country house did not, was a yard that I could do half a dozen flips in to get to the other side.

Behind the business adjoining our home, was a large yard with a horseshoe pit. This area would end up being the scene for dozens of happy memories. There were barbeques, pig roasts, my little brother's graduation party, and where mom would hold dozens of yard sales in the connected front yard to our house. When the yard was not thrumming with activity, it was a quiet place that I could hide and get away. It's definitely a place that I miss and am grateful for having when I did.

The house was spacious enough to allow my mother to begin watching a few neighborhood children for some additional, albeit meager, income. This eventually grew into her having a licensed day-care that she ran out of our home. This new house was not large by any means, but we were all able to live comfortably within its walls. On the other side of the wooden front door was a concrete porch, framed by a brick flowerbed, and a concrete sidewalk that led about a hundred feet to the front door of the veterinary hospital, whose brick flowerbeds matched ours perfectly. Behind the house were not the fields I had grown so fond of, but five acres of forest that would come to have its own fair share of stories. Playing in the woods or the river behind our new home became one of my most treasured places. Children of all ages would find their way to this magical spot and we would spend hours building forts and dams. I always felt free and safe to play and explore in that space with no limitations or boundaries. The possibilities there seemed endless as though time and space were infinite.

I would often visit the veterinary clinic growing up, running next door when there were no clients to visit with whichever vet assistant was there that day. Occasionally, my godfather would be there, but his time was usually taken up attending to the animals. I do remember sometimes when he would take me into the animal rooms and introduce me to some of the current 'guests.' I remember that where the dog kennels were toward the back were smelly and loud, but I still enjoyed my time there. Somewhere I have a Polaroid picture of me playing inside one of the cat cages, looking out from between the bars, in a Halloween cat costume. I must have been around 4 years old. When I was around nine or ten, I started to help mom clean out the animal's cages and close the building for the evening. As I got older, I started to mow the clinic's lawn that was connected to our own.

Some of the fondest memories I have living next to a veterinary hospital was getting to own so many of the cats that people would drop off on the property. My guess is that they were hoping the veterinarian would find them and take them in. We would often hear tiny meows coming from the wood pile or from the blackberry bushes behind the house; new residents alerting us to their presence. Over the years, some of the animals became family. There was Toot-Toot, who must have been close to a hundred in cat years. Popcorn was another cat, named for his affinity for jumping up repeatedly to peak through our windows. If Suck-Face were ever behind you on the couch or snuggled up to your neck, you would better grab some tissues because you were about to be soaked by his drool. Being able to interact with these animals helped foster a life-long love of animals, especially cats with quirky personalities.

Shortly after settling into our new home, we went on a family road-trip from Washington to Idaho. I learned along the way that the purpose of this trip was to pick up my big brother. I remember the joy and excitement I felt. My older brother was sixteen, about ten years my senior, and his momma used to be married to our daddy a long time ago. These details never mattered too much to me as I just saw him as my beloved older brother, of whom I was proud to call mine. I was bursting with happiness when I finally saw him outside the car window, surrounded by a handful of other tall, teenage boys. Seeing my big brother there, knowing that he was going to come home to live with us, which was a beautiful memorable moment. Not so beautiful was that shortly after this pick up, I threw up in the back seat of the car. Dang! That was not the impression I was going for.

A funny note to this story is that after I gave my older brother this book to read before publishing it, he laughed and told me that he had *no idea* I had thought about him this way growing up. His memory of that day differed from mine as well. He told me that he didn't actually come home with us that day. He had stayed in Idaho for a few days, wrapping up loose ends, and then hopped a bus to Washington. We picked him up from the bus stop, about fifteen minutes from our home. So that was an interesting conversation I enjoyed.

Despite our age difference, we were able to bond over shared interests. I have fond memories of him introducing me to Elton John's music, of which I grew to love. We would listen to his records on dads' phonograph. He introduced me to The Hobbit and its fantasy world of heroes struggling and triumphing against powerful foes. When I developed an interest in World War II history, particularly the history of the holocaust, he was there to discuss it with me, sharing the fascination and horror in exploring humanity's capacity for evil. He could always explain math and history better than the encyclopedias I would have to go through. As I grew into a teenager and actively avoided my family members most days, I would make an exception to greet him when I heard him come home. I will always be grateful for having a big brother like him.

4

CONFUSION

"Child sexual abuse cuts across all social classes and racial and religious groups. Both boys and girls are victimized, and it is not a very rare occurrence. Our best estimates suggest that, by the age of 18, one in every four females and one of seven males have been subjected to some form of contact sexual abuse. Child sexual abuse is, by its very nature, secretive. It almost always occurs when a child is alone with an offender. In order for the sexual activity to continue, offenders rely on the children to keep the secret."[5]

Much of my childhood was like any other, at least, I assume in many ways, it was. Memories can be slippery things, wriggling out of our line of sight when we try to focus on the painful parts. The loss of time and details from my memories is overwhelming and frustrating. I wish I could say with certainty, 'Mom and Dad went out and I was being babysat,' I have hazy, nightmarish memories and questions without answers.

Looking back as an adult, I can see that so much of how I behaved was related to what I had experienced and was at a loss of how to communicate. I was awkward around peers, obsessive and ritualistic with many routines, and was frequently deprived of sleep from the nightmares. I was very neurotic for a child, interacting with my toys in an incredibly careful manner, anxious to hurt or upset them. When I colored, I would not

---

[5] Ibid., 305.

stop until the picture was completely colored-in, not wanting to offend or disappoint the image left partially un-colored. If I outlined a character in a coloring book, I apologized for having to touch their privates[6].

I would often have toileting accidents at home, at school, and when we traveled, which reinforced my self-consciousness. I didn't know how to ask for help with words. I remember one night that I squatted in the middle of my bed, urinated down my legs, then lied back down. I cried until one of my parents came into my room, they'd comfort me, for what they had assumed was another nightmare. The mistrust I felt toward others was mistaken for shyness. I tried to stay unnoticed, not wanting to catch unwanted attention, unintentionally depriving myself of the acknowledgement and support I so desperately needed.

It was 1977 and I was eight years old. This is when I had the first encounter with an individual I will refer to as Abuser B.

I remember sitting in Dad's big, comfy recliner, partially perched on Abuser B's lap, both of us watching what was on the television. He started touching me lightly between my legs, whispering, "Do you like this? Don't make a noise." Confused and alarmed, my mind raced as he continued to speak softly to me, holding me still in that position. *Why is he touching my private area? Should I try to jump off the chair? He says that I will like this. Am I supposed to like this? Should I call out? I'm supposed to listen to him. He says I should be quiet. I'm supposed to stay quiet.* From that point onward, whenever he would catch me alone, it would be like that. He touched my private parts, told me not to say a word, and I would grapple with the horrible feelings of confusion, guilt, and fear. I couldn't escape. I had to stay quiet.

There was a small room in our home that was eventually turned into an extension for the kitchen. Before the remodel, I claimed that room as my bedroom for a short time. The walls were painted a dark purple. I was lying on my side, facing the wall. It was nighttime and I was trying to fall asleep. I heard him enter this small, private space and felt the bed shift as he lied down next to me, also facing the wall. I laid as still as I could, frozen

---

[6] "Traumatized people find themselves reenacting some aspect of the trauma scene in disguised form, without realizing what they are doing." Herman, *Trauma and Recovery*, 40.

in terror at the strangeness of this encounter. I felt him pull my underwear down. He positioned himself, as if to put himself between my legs. I stared at a spot on the wall where the purple paint had been chipped away, leaving the light blue clown wallpaper behind it exposed. All I could do was focus on this spot, my consciousness narrowing to exclude everything but this tiny spot on my bedroom wall. That was all I could do.[7] I was powerless to escape him. I changed bedrooms; he still came in. I hid to avoid him; he sought me out. I was confused and afraid all the time.

A seemingly innocuous memory from this time is an image of a package on our kitchen table. The package was addressed to Abuser B, his name clearly spelled out along with our home's address. This image, this crystal-clear identification of that man who hurt me so much, is still seared into my memory like a brand forty years later.[8]

This man continued to be in and out of our house for a year or so. Eventually, my behaviors changed. I clearly recall one encounter where I shook my booty at him as he walked by. After all these years, that memory remains disturbingly clear. It is because of this small action that years later, as I was being told that it wasn't my fault, I did not believe that to be true. I wanted to have some control, some sliver of autonomy. This was the lesson I learned of how to take control of these situations: you can't have something taken from you if you are offering to give away.

---

[7] "Dissociation is the essence of trauma. The overwhelming experience is split off and fragmented, so that the emotions, sounds, images, thoughts, and physical sensations related to the trauma take on a life of their own. The sensory fragments of memory intrude into the present, where they are literally relived. As long as the trauma is not resolved, the stress hormones that the body secretes to protect itself keep circulating, and the defensive movements and emotional responses keep getting replayed." Van der Kolk, *The Body Keeps the Score: Brain, Mind, and Body in the Healing of Trauma*, 66.

[8] "It is as if time stops at the moment of trauma. The traumatic moment becomes encoded in an abnormal form of memory, which breaks spontaneously into consciousness, both as flashbacks during waking states and as traumatic nightmares during sleep." Herman, *Trauma and Recovery*, 37.

5

FIRST DISCLOSURE

"Because of the secretive nature of sexual abuse and the wide range of children's behavioral reactions, child sexual abuse is a difficult problem to detect. Children who have been sexually abused, however, are most often identified as a result of their own accidental or purposeful disclosures. Some children accidently reveal their abuse by exhibiting adult-like sexual behaviors or by sharing sexual knowledge that is beyond their years. Some children may make a vague disclosure to a friend, who then tells an adult. Parents should be aware of sudden changes in behavior: nightmares; withdrawal and avoidance of particular persons, places, or things; and unusual aggressiveness, jumpiness, and/or inappropriate sexual behavior."[9]

My silence broke eventually. I was turning ten and had several girls over for a sleepover, presumably to celebrate my birthday. All of us giggly little girls lied in a circle, cozy in our sleeping bags, talking about all the things little girls talk about at sleepovers. During this happy interaction, surrounded by my peers, the feelings of loneliness and fear that had defined so much of the past year lifted. I was overcome by the sudden and urgent need to disclose what had happened to me.

My memory of what I told my friends slips quickly into me retreating into my sleeping bag, covering my head, and avoiding what I assume to

---

[9] Cohen et al., *Treating Trauma and Traumatic Grief in Children and Adolescents*, 306.

be the worried looks from my friends. This memory then turns into my mother asking me a lot of questions the next morning, her face serious and alarmed. I cannot remember what I told her verbatim, but I know it was enough for her to understand what had happened to me.

Shortly after my disclosure, I was told that Abuser B was going to be 'taken care of.' At the time, I had assumed this meant that my daddy and big brother had buried him six-feet-deep somewhere. This assumption made me feel safe and protected from any chance of that man hurting me again. I was honestly disappointed to find out as a teenager that he had not in fact been killed and buried in the woods, and that 'taken care of' meant something else entirely. He had essentially been told to leave and not come back. It felt better when I thought he was dead.

6

MOVING FORWARD

"Initiation, intimidation, stigmatization, isolation, helplessness and self-blame depend on a terrifying reality of child sexual abuse... "Don't worry about things like that; that could never happen in our family." "How could you ever think of such a terrible thing?" "Don't let me ever hear you say anything like that again!" The average child never asks and never tells."[10]

Life moved forward and I carried my pain and confusion forward with me. Despite this, I was still able to maintain friendships and enjoy being a child most of the time. I have many happy memories playing with my friends as a ten- and eleven-year-old. We let our imaginations run free. We played pretend and became characters from our favorite books and movies. We would play as though Sandy and Budd from the television show Flipper were our boyfriends. We would talk about how cute they were and how much they adored us, further establishing ourselves into their world. Sometimes we would take the aluminum rowboat out on the lake. Other days, we would pack a picnic to eat before jumping off the dock to swim. We would chase the 'treasure' shining on the water's surface, eager for the chance to find our own gold. We never did end up catching it. We were also fond of playing Nancy Drew. I loved Nancy Drew books and read them whenever I got the chance. I adored get swept up in the intrigue

---

[10] Roland C. Summit, "The Child Sexual Abuse Accomodation Syndrome," *Child Abuse & Neglect* 7, no. 2 (1983): pp. 177-193, https://doi.org/10.1016/0145-2134(83)90070-4.

and excitement of solving mysteries. Pulling from my knowledge of the books, we made our very own 'mystery kits.' After our kits were packed, we would set off to the forest to solve our own mysteries.

Our favorite game to play was to imagine that we were the Ingalls girls. Little House on the Prairie was by far our favorite show and being surrounded by the wild outdoors with its spacious fields provided the perfect place to play as Mary and Laura. I was drawn to their story, to the simple, honest lives filled with adventures in a natural setting that was reminiscent of my own surroundings. I found it interesting how much school had changed since then. No longer were all the town's children together in the same room, all ages, sharing the workspace with two to a desk. We would act out the daily lives of Laura and Mary, pretending to fetch water from a well, wash clothes in the lake, or sewing our own clothes. Sometimes our play went outside the realm of imagination, as I remember us actually re-creating the aprons that Ma Ingalls would wear.

I enjoyed reading about the people the Ingalls girls would talk to in town. I particularly enjoyed reading about when Laura would go to Nell's Mercantile, a general store, to trade her farm's eggs for provisions. Mrs. Olson, who ran the store with her husband, would make snide remarks to Laura about what her family already owed. Right at that moment, Mr. Olson would save Laura from humiliation by interrupting his wife with a clever retort, making her gasp and fall silent, bested for now. The kindly Mr. Olson would then give Laura the items she traded for, plus some candy from the big glass jars as a bonus. The more I read and re-read the story, the more I felt a part of their world. It always made me feel good when Laura and Mary learned important lessons; from farming and hard work, to loving your neighbor and the concept of death, there were so many things about life that I learned from those books.

7

NOT A STRANGER

"Little is known about the mind of the perpetrator. His most consistent feature, in both the testimony of his victims and the observations of psychologists, is his apparent normality. Ordinary concepts of psychopathology fail to define of comprehend him. This idea is deeply disturbing to most people. How much more comforting it would be if the perpetrator were easily recognizable, obviously deviant or disturbed. But he is not."[11]

My childhood brought me to encounter a man, in a small cabin, not too far from home. When I would visit the residence, (liability reasons permits me from providing the connection as to whom I was visiting.) I remember feeling like we were back in frontier times. The one-room building was run-down and a bit shabby that provided insects little resistance for visiting us unannounced. The interior contained a modest assortment of furniture including a wood stove, a card table that was all-purpose, and a daybed where her dad slept. It felt so different from my daily life there. At the cabin, we were free to explore the woods and the lake without much oversight, a noticeable difference from the restrictions at home. I imagined this was how Laura and Mary had felt—free and one with the land. One night, we fell asleep playing under the cabin's kitchen table. After we woke up, we were told we were heard talking in our

---

[11] Cohen et al., *Treating Trauma and Traumatic Grief in Children and Adolescents*, 75.

sleep. We had been talking to each other as if we were the Ingalls sisters, addressing each other as Mary and Laura.

There was no running water at the cabin, so to brush our teeth, we used a cup of water from a bottle, or a pot boiled on the stove. We would then spit our used-up foamy toothpaste over the railing of the large balcony that surrounded a good portion of the back of the cabin. This balcony was also useful for dumping the contents of the large red Folger's coffee can if we chose not to use the trees or the outhouse to do our business at night. The outhouse was my least favorite thing about the cabin. It was a cramped, dark enclosure that stunk worse than anything I had ever smelled in my whole life. It was home to many spiders, their many webs strategically located within the outhouse to catch the flies that were drawn to the powerful stench. As repellant as the spiders and stench, were the walls of the outhouse. They were covered in dingy pages torn out of Playboy magazines. I had been aware that her daddy had these magazines laying around various places where he would spend his time, like his truck. When we would find them, we would open them and gawk at the images for a minute or two before returning to our play. Sitting in the outhouse, I looked at the suggestive and erotic images, feeling a passing curiosity about the women in the photographs. More than anything, the presence of these pictures validated my developing beliefs about the needs of men. I kept my visits to the outhouse as infrequent as possible.

Mostly, the memories I have at the cabin were happy and fun. Since there was no running water, we had to go into town to wash clothes. Trips to the laundry mat were always a small adventure. The laundry mat was modest and had just one small room with a few washing machines on the floor and a few dryers lining one wall. There were two chairs in the corner next to a small table with magazines laying in a messy pile. We would play with dolls or read books while enjoying the smell of the detergent as the clothes were being washed.

We made our own fun at the cabin. I remember one time when my friend and I decided to play in the back of her daddy's work truck, as we would do from time-to-time. We often took our lunches with us when playing in the truck. Once, we decided to dig through the truck's ashtray. We found some tiny cigarette butts and smoked them, always glancing over our shoulders to make sure we would not get caught. Emboldened by our mischief, we found some small twigs and tried to smoke those too, with far less success.

On days that the weather prevented us from spending all day outside, we would be lifted up into the loft where we slept and played indoors. The loft was as shabby as the rest of the cabin, created by plywood being laid across the beams that supported the building's structure. Up in the loft was where all the dolls and coloring books were, and we would spend hours playing in this cozy space that was just for us. I remember how odd it was when my friend's daddy explained to us that his back hurt too much to lift us into the loft. He told us that for tonight, we would have to sleep on the main floor. We were given the corner of the cabin that had a comfy chair in which we could sit, read, or play games until it was time to sleep.

At bedtime, he instructed my friend to sleep in the corner space and that I would take the daybed. The next memory I have after lying down to sleep was sensing this man lying down behind me. I must have been dozing off because I do not have a clear memory of him getting into the bed. Confused and barely awake, I felt him put his hands in my underwear. This scared me enough to start crying, the commotion waking my friend. My memories go fuzzy here and I cannot remember the immediate reaction to what happened, just that I was taken home. I never saw the cabin again and shortly after what happened, my friend moved to another state with her mom.

I did end up seeing Abuser C, again. Our town was small, so it was hard to avoid him entirely. I watched him walking all over town, for years. I had learned from my previous experiences with being molested that the only thing I could do to protect myself was to try to stay away from him. He came to my parents' home after my mom passed, years later. I guess he thought that showing up right after my mother's funeral service would be a good time to drum up some business. I was standing in the yard with my first husband when he arrived. I had shared the story of what happened in the cabin with my husband previously, so when that man came closer to us, he asked me if that was the guy who molested me. After I confirmed that he was, my husband immediately walked part way across the yard, shouting at him to 'get the fuck off the property.' As distressing as it was to see that man again, it felt empowering to have my husband's support in defending me. Perhaps it was the acknowledgement that this man was told, out-loud (as if he needed to be reminded), that he was not welcome here.

I would later ask myself, *did this man get in trouble for what he did? Did he hurt my friend too?* Thinking back on this friend, I think that she was actually the one who told my parents about what I had disclosed at the slumber party a couple years before. In a way, she helped protect me twice by communicating with words what I could not. Unfortunately for me, her disclosure this time led to me losing her. Once again, a friend had moved away after I was molested by a man that we trusted, never knowing if I was truly alone in my nightmarish experience, or if they too had known nightmares like mine.

8

THE PEER EXPERIENCE

"Our society's un-comfortabilities with sex limits our capacity to prevent [sexual abuse]. These attitudes may be responsible for keeping it hidden."[12]

By the time I was eleven, I had been exposed to a lot of sexual behaviors. So, it was around this time that I had begun to masturbate, reenacting how others had touched me.[13] I had made quite a habit of it, often self-stimulating until it felt like my arms would fall right off. I remember one time when I was on the couch, around the corner from the kitchen where my mom and her friends sat, talking about whatever moms and their friends talked about. I must have been making some noise because I heard my mother's voice call out, "Are you laughing in there?" I immediately stopped what I was doing, feeling my cheeks burn with shame, and was silent from then on. The shame I felt reinforced the lesson that anything to do with sex was a secret and it was my responsibility to be silent about it. As an adult, I regret that this undoubtedly awkward moment was not recognized by my mother as a cry for help. Here again, I was waving my arms from behind a window, signaling for aid. Once more, my behaviors were acknowledged and yet somehow still unnoticed.

Despite the, disconnect between my parent's understanding, and what I had experienced, I still felt a deep, secure attachment to them. They loved

---

[12] Ibid., 305.

[13] "The reenactment of traumatic scenes is most apparent in the repetitive play of children." Ibid., 39.

me very much and I carry fond, beautiful memories of both of them with me always. Some of my favorite memories with dad were when we would lie down on the ground in the backyard, look at the stars, and just talk. The sky and stars were so beautiful and as a child, I believed that they were as magical as they were lovely. During my childhood, dad's job kept him from home often. Spending quiet, alone time with just me and dad was a rare occurrence, made even more special for its rarity.

My favorite memories of mom were also of her spending time with me—just us girls. I loved talking with her, watching television together, shopping, and going on long drives with me in the front seat. She always spoke with me with respect and helped demonstrate what it meant to treat people respectfully too. If I had something to say, I rarely felt like I was going to be judged or criticized by her. Her heart and her love were unconditional. I always got the impression that she enjoyed our special time together as much as I did. I appreciate those memories even more since she has passed. To me, those memories have a very real kind of magic. They helped outline a legacy for me to carry forward. Following her example, I carried the magic of her kindness, compassion, and respect with me during my time caring for the children in my life. Whether they were my own biological children or children who were entrusted to my care, I did my best to follow the example of my mother's loving actions.

9

SUNDAY SCHOOL TRIP

"Although a small percentage of sex offenders are women, the majority is male. Sex offenders are generally *not* "dirty old men" or strangers lurking in alleys. In fact, sex offenders are often well known and trusted by the children they abuse. There is no clear-cut description or profile of a sex offender, and there is no way to recognize a potential abuser."[14]

Throughout my childhood, my family and I regularly attended church. We went to the services and participated in church functions with the other members. My favorite part of church was Sunday school. In Sunday school, we would sing hymns, make art, have snacks, and play while the grown-ups attended services. I never had to worry when I was in Sunday school. It was a happy, safe place. Sunday school also provided its members the opportunity to go on trips together. All the kids would pile into a bus and off we'd go. I would sit by my girlfriends and we would talk and joke to pass the time.

I was about thirteen when we went on a cross-country skiing trip. Cross-country skiing was not something that thirteen-year-old me thought would be enjoyable. I was not particularly athletic and learned that it was certainly harder work than it looked. After we had finished the grueling test of endurance cross-country skiing turned out to be, we went in the ski lodge to rest. We congregated around the huge, round fire pit in the

---

[14] Ibid., 305.

center of the building, peeling off wet mittens and warming ourselves by the fire. As is the nature of the newly pubescent, I was on high alert for any boys who might be cute. My gaze darted furtively around the fire pit, noticing who was noticing me.

As the youth group climbed back onto the bus to return home, I chose to sit with an older boy instead of my friends. I felt excited and nervous, my new teen hormones inspiring boldness in the hope of making a meaningful connection. We were seated closer to the front of the bus than to the back, within eyesight of the driver. It was not long into the drive that the boy and I were making out. It started with light kisses and quickly escalated into open-mouth tongue kissing. I wanted to keep pace with this older boy and show him that I was willing to do what he wanted, what was expected of me as a girl. The kissing continued to be hot and heavy and the next thing I knew, he had his hand down the front of my pants. I remember him shushing me, telling me to be quiet. My mind made the connection—this was a sex-thing; I was supposed to be quiet and to keep it a secret. As an adult, it is hard to understand exactly how all this occurred without comment or intervention from an adult in this semi-public space. It seems like such an obvious display of over-sexualization—an older boy molesting a thirteen-year-old on the way home from a Sunday school trip. Here, again, I was visible and overlooked.

Within the same year, my parents took me to a local river to be baptized. It was a beautiful, bright day, perfect for an outdoor event. I felt nervous, but excited, and maybe a little overwhelmed. Our family had many close relationships with church members and friends from town, and the sizable turnout for my baptism was proof of their support. Many of the attendees stood on river rocks around the baptism site, cheerfully watching me approach the river with the pastor. Thankfully, I remember the water was not too cold that day. The pastor was vigilant in my preparation for the ritual. He made sure that I understood what would happen during the baptism, and that I knew what to do. Then it was time—arms crossed, plugged nose, tipped back and fully submerged, then brought back up above the water to my feet. A few deep breaths later, and I walked back to where my mother stood, a fully baptized member of our church. After we went home, I remember feeling proud, but exhausted. Mom and I talked about the event and what it meant to me. I wish that I could remember her exact words from that day, to be able to recall with perfect clarity the conversations about faith and meaning we shared. Looking back on that moment in my life, I find it ironic that this beautiful rite of passage did nothing to protect me from spiraling into drug use and self-destructive behaviors shortly after.

10

M Y   B O D Y   A N D   M E

"This is not—devastatingly—an uncommon event after trauma: the way an individual experiences their body is ruptured, distorted, painful, humiliating. In many individuals, eating disorders and self-harm are not only ways of expressing such ruptures of the self and body, but are also a result of it: self-harm is an individual's physical demonstration of their relationship with their body, their self."[15]

My trauma began to affect my life in more obvious ways as I grew into a young woman. As a child, the anxiety of being in potentially unsafe situations and the compulsive behaviors that I thought could keep me safe had generalized to a pronounced fear of physical harm. Due to the long-term effects of traumatic experiences on the adrenal system, my startle response had become exaggerated.[16] This meant that I was 'jumpy' and quick to assume that danger was near. Sounds like doors slamming, people yelling, and other loud, sudden noises easily triggered an amygdala flood,

---

[15] Kesherie Gurung, "Bodywork: Self-Harm, Trauma, and Embodied Expressions of Pain," *Arts and Humanities in Higher Education* 17, no. 1 (December 2018): pp. 32-47, https://doi.org/10.1177/1474022216684634, 37.

[16] "After a traumatic experience, the human system of self-preservation seems to go onto permanent alert, as if the danger might return at any moment. Physiological arousal continues unabated. In this state of hyperarousal, [...] the traumatized person startles easily, reacts irritably to small provocations, and sleeps poorly." Cohen et al., *Treating Trauma and Traumatic Grief in Children and Adolescents*, 35.

i.e., a full activation of the fight-flight-freeze response. It was hard for me to self-sooth as a child, and it was often difficult to calm down after experiencing such powerful emotions.

The news was terrifying and any mention of people dying or getting hurt had the potential to trigger crying bouts. I assume that my parents just thought it was because I was an empathetic kid, sensitive to the suffering of others. They were not wrong, I suppose. I had also been disturbed by watching "The Day After," a movie about a nuclear strike on the United States. The movie is categorized as drama and science-fiction, but during the 1980's, the threat of nuclear war and felt very real. This movie preyed upon my brain's tendency toward generating negative cognitions, another hallmark symptom of post-traumatic stress.[17] I had already had the tendency by this point to imagine catastrophic outcomes, believing that the worst-case scenario was the most likely to happen. This movie brought an apocalyptic worst-case scenario to life right on my home's television screen.

My lifetime journey with anorexia nervosa and a severely negative body self-image has been exhausting, even as a child. Before I had even begun preadolescence, I had established a complicated relationship with food. I cannot remember ever having much of an appetite. I have early memories of not liking food and of being labeled a picky eater, a label that has stuck with me to this day. When I was a child, the attention I received from not eating caused me to feel ashamed. This sense of shame in association with eating strengthened my avoidance to food. Being called name calling by adults didn't help either. This was one of Abuser C's favorite names to call me. The uncomfortable feelings about this name transformed into a humiliating label in my mind, promoting significant embarrassment and avoidance to eating among peers.

I have a memory of being around nine years old one of the times my mother addressed my eating habits. I had a general awareness of my body then. I was skinny, but not too skinny, with no breasts, and felt deeply uncomfortable in my own skin. When I ate very little, as was typical, my mom would joke—but not really joke—that if I continued to not eat, I would have to go to the hospital. There, they would have to put a needle in my arm to feed me. She was aware of my deathly fear of needles and

---

[17] Herman, *Trauma and Recovery,* 28-29.

hoped my aversion to *them* would outweigh my aversion to finishing my meal. This not-so-subtle threat was effective for maybe another bite or two before my mother gave up, exasperated by my unwillingness to eat.

I began binging and purging before sixth grade. I had arrived at the age when I began to deeply crave boys' romantic attention. My experiences with intimacy and sexuality had been warped by this time from trauma, but despite all of that, I still craved human connection.[18] Consciously or unconsciously, I had come to understand that my body is what was liked—what brought people close. At the time, I had no idea how wrong this way of thinking was. I rarely felt 'good enough', and I took my feelings of inadequacy out on my physical form. The bulimic behaviors were eventually noticed by my mother, and she intervened. She explained to me how the vomiting hurt my teeth and my insides and if I kept making myself throw up, the damage would get worse and worse. This was enough of a deterrent to end my binging and purging, but not enough to disrupt the connections I had made between food, my body, and my self-worth.

Once I got to be a young adult, I began to appreciate my strong, athletic form. A part of me still acknowledged that this body was what I had to offer—it was my worth. I still struggled with insecurities about having a small chest. I had always been extremely self-conscious about that part of me. I still cried over not liking my body's shape, as I had throughout middle and high school. I know now that my general non-acceptance of my body influenced my lack of self-respect, and why I had allowed my body to be used by others so often. Even as I aged into full adulthood, my negative body-image did not weaken much. When I progressed through my forties, I faced another challenge—a slowing metabolism that affected my ability to stay thin as easily as before. I was too scared to further damage my teeth's enamel or the lining of my stomach to binge and purge, so I chose the alternative of severely restricting my food intake. I survived on a handful of carbs, sugar-laden juices, sodas, and the caffeination of coffee and tea for a while. During that time, people would often compliment my figure, never knowing how unhealthy I was—emotionally and physically.

Through therapy and the help of my supports, I have begun to lean into the unknown of getting older. I certainly could do better, but I am

---

[18] "Trauma impels people both to withdraw from close relationships and to seek them desperately." Ibid., 56.

more intentional about eating regularly and eating healthily. People still like to give me a hard time during meals about what I have or have not eaten. I know now, however, that the only one who needs to know what I eat is me. To be fair, the servings at restaurants are huge and do hardly looked touched by the time I have eaten my fill. That just means I get to take home leftovers for lunch the next day. I still feel like this area is a work in progress, but I'm grateful for my growth and the opportunities I've had to learn to like myself.

11

OUTCAST

"Abused children generally discover at some point in their development that they can produce major, though temporary, alterations in their affective state by voluntarily inducing autonomic crises or extreme autonomic arousal. Purging and vomiting, compulsive sexual behavior, compulsive risk taking or exposure to danger, and the use of psychoactive drugs become the vehicles by which abused children attempt to regulate their internal emotional states. Through these devices, abused children attempt to obliterate their chronic dysphoria and to stimulate, however briefly, an internal state of well-being and comfort that cannot otherwise be achieved. These self-destructive symptoms are often well established in abused children even before adolescence, and they become much more prominent in the adolescent years."[19]

I remember being so excited to start my seventh-grade year. This was the first year of middle school and the building was just for seventh and eighth grade students. I went to registration with mom. She helped me navigate the chaos of registering for classes and asked me about what extracurriculars I was interested in exploring. I remember enthusiastically signing up for various clubs, my optimism for this new chapter in my life inspiring me to participate in a handful of fun-sounding programs. This

---

[19] Ibid., 109-110.

optimism was short-lived, unfortunately. The anticipation of walking into a club's first meeting quickly pivoted to feeling awkward—like I didn't belong there with the other kids. I did not want to go back after that.

Around this time, I had developed a sense of being different from the other students, even my friends from elementary school. It wasn't obvious to me why I was different now. These were the girls that were my best friends. We had gone to Brownies together, had sleepovers, celebrated our birthdays every year as a group. Without cause or warning, I was unceremoniously cast out of our little circle, ignored by my peers. My feelings of confusion and grief over the loss of my friends quickly transmuted to anger and contempt. *How the hell are they 'popular' while I'm shit?* The anger overshadowed the hurt most days. On days that the rejection stung too much to bear, I would make myself sick or fake some ailment so I could stay home from school. Playing hooky provided a temporary respite from the constant heartache I felt.

During my time middle school, my anxiety and hurt had developed into something darker. It felt as though I was still jumping and waving my hands behind that same window I had been standing behind since I was five years old, and I was getting desperate. I began to behave in a way I had hoped would draw some attention. I thought that maybe if I behaved badly enough, I could get someone to see how much pain I was in and then maybe, finally, I would be offered some help. At the time I was twelve, maybe thirteen, I was already smoking marijuana, skipping classes, hitchhiking from town to town, and jumping on city buses that took me all over the general area. When my feelings of shame and confusion overwhelmed me, I would scratch and pinch my skin with my fingernails or a paperclip until marks appeared. The sharp physical pain distracted me, taking the pressure off the emotional anguish, if only for a little while. I would be anxious for others to see the marks, wanting them to be seen, but not wanting it to be obvious. Occasionally, I would make sure that the marks were visible when I was around my mom or friends. Nothing was ever said to me, my self-injuries were never addressed. I continued to try different ways to get noticed behind the wall of dirty glass that separated me from everyone else.

I became more and more reckless regarding my safety. I did drugs, was promiscuous, battled an eating disorder, and put myself in all sorts of dangerous situations during my teens. Scratching my skin escalated into punching walls and cars, bringing a whole new level of pain. Most of the actual damage done by this was to my wrist. The injuries I sustained led me to having to wear a wrist-brace for months a few times during my teens—after every time I punched something hard enough to hurt myself. My lack of self-respect and disregard for my health was something I could control; it was something I *chose*. I could not be made to think less of myself if I already thought I was worthless. I could not be made to suffer by another's hand if I were already suffering by mine. I took this pain and folded it onto myself.

12

LOVE OF ROCK & ROLL

"In the aftermath of an experience of overwhelming danger, the two contradictory responses of intrusion and construction establish an oscillating rhythm. This dialectic of opposing psychological states is perhaps the most characteristic feature of the post-traumatic syndromes. Since neither the intrusive nor the numbing symptoms allow for integration of the traumatic event, the alternation between these two extreme states might be understood as an attempt to find a satisfactory balance between the two. But balance is precisely what the traumatized person lacks. She finds herself caught between the extremes of amnesia or of reliving the trauma, between floods of intense, overwhelming feeling and arid states of no feeling at all, between irritable, impulsive action and complete inhibition of action."[20]

I am proud to say that I was able to find some good friends along the way. Throughout middle and high school, I had two best-friends, both of whom were huge parts of my life. I did not typically hang out with both friends at the same time, but they were each present in my life. I would not have traded them for all the friends in the world.

Part of the way through seventh grade, we were introduced to stimulants. Caffeine pills or speed became my drugs of choice, aside from

---

[20] Ibid., 47.

marijuana. It was fun to experience the intense burst of energy and feeling extra hyper and silly. The pills also reduced my appetite, allowing me to eat even less than I did already. I had no bad intentions for my health or safety when taking these drugs. I was just a seventh grader who had no idea what the hell she was doing. I remember one day at school, while I was under the influence of these pills, channeling my amplified energy into swinging on the heavy metal school doors. I jumped up to grab the top of the door and used my momentum to swing back and forth. A few hours later, I called my mom to come and get me because I was 'sick.' The comedown from the pills did not feel good of course, when I got home, I was sent to bed to rest. As I tried to lie down to relax, I realized that my body was not prepared to stop moving at that point. After my mom had left my room, I got up and danced around wildly, working out the energetic impulses inspired by the stimulants that were not quite out of my system at that time. Finally, from either boredom or exhaustion, I eventually passed out.

By eighth grade, I was doing little more than partying. My emerging identity differentiated me from the girls I had once called friends. I began to resent the snotty girls running around, making shitty little comments when they would walk by. Giving me mean looks that I swear I could feel on my back as I walked away from them. One afternoon that I was just done with it—done with all their shit. I was walking down the hallway between classes and I saw one of these girls. We sang in choir together, and we had said some words during class that day. I saw her walking down the hall in the opposite direction as me. I met her with a left punch to the gut. I was able to land a few more blows before being walked to the principal's office. At that point, the violence I had been inflicting upon myself began to turn outward as well.

At about thirteen, I attended one of my little brother's sports events. I remember looking around, taking in the environment, when I noticed this kid to my left. He was a little older than me and riding his bike in the nearby schoolyard. Not long after I started watching him, this kid flips his bike on a log and goes ass over tea kettle. Clearly not discouraged, he then got up and tried the whole thing over again. I can't clearly remember if his stunt was successful, but I do remember that after his attempts, he made his way over to me to strike up a conversation. I later learned that his bike-stunts were in hopes of impressing me. Something must have worked because we began to date soon after. Three years later, when I was a freshman in high school, I remember waiting for him to come pick me up from my parents. As I waited outside, I started to hear sirens. Not long after that, I found out that he had just been in a motorcycle accident behind our house. He had been hurt in the accident and was put in a body-cast. The entire summer he was in that cast I helped take care of him.

I was a junior in high school when he left to join the service. I gave him a Dear John letter and we ended our relationship. I found out some time later that he went on to marry and have a family. It was tragic to learn that not long after building his new life, he was killed in another motorcycle accident. Shortly after my Dear John letter, I learned that a different middle-school boyfriend had unexpectedly died—a different motorcycle accident. Later that year, I went on a few dates with another young man, only to attend his funeral the following year. He was killed in an accident when a semi-truck ran through a stoplight. The funeral was overwhelming for me. His leather jacket was placed on top of his casket. I had worn that jacket. I knew what it smelled like. I could not bear to be in the church for more than five minutes before I had to run out. It was all too much.

School continued to be a struggle, needless to say. My awkwardness and insecurities combined with unresolved trauma led me to overcompensate with negative, unhealthy behaviors. Mostly all the moments I had with my friends were great. We explored our world and self-sabotaged with one another, creating many unforgettable memories. Throughout all our adventures together, a strong sense of loyalty and kinship was formed. I started middle school with a friend with whom we embraced and encouraged each other's wildness, turning up Ozzy Osbourne's "Crazy Train" in the middle of the common area. Away from school, we sometimes found ourselves in some compromising situations. When we were spending our time innocently, we could be found singing along to Joan Jett in my bedroom, complete with fully choreography. Our mutual love of music led us to the underground concert scene, but our first concert was with my dad. He took us to a Billy Joel concert in Seattle when we were thirteen. We sat close to the nosebleed section and loved every minute of it, the first of many concerts to follow.

This friend went to a family reunion with me, to a quaint little place in Oregon one year. We walked all over town and spent time at the river down the hill from the building where the reunion was held. We practiced boxing for a few minutes as we stood by the water. *Where* was *the best place to land the first punch? The gut? The chin?* Thankfully, our practices didn't lead to any significant injuries and we mostly just spent our time walking around town as much as possible.

Around the end of middle and beginning of high school, I made friends with another girl in my class. We met at school and found out that we had almost everything in common. We would walk down the railroad tracks next to the school after going to the nearby convenient store where we loaded ourselves up with candy and soda. We would often walk over to the other side of town to the old train cars that remained stationary and accessible in the infrequently visited train yard. Occasionally, one of our favorite cars would have a bottle of whiskey or a bag of weed stashed away. To this day, those old train cars still sit in the same place. The area is caged off now.

This friend's mother must have been an amazingly brave woman because she decided to take us to Reno when we were fifteen. Things were different back then, but it still seems like a daunting task trying to wrangle two teenage girls in an exciting and unfamiliar place like Reno. I remember that our flight there was one of the only times that flying did not faze me. Perhaps I was experiencing some feelings of adolescent invulnerability, or maybe just the overwhelming excitement drowned out any anxiety. The lights, of course, were amazing and at that time I had never seen anything like it. Despite my friend's mom's efforts in reigning us in, I was having none of it. Carrying on with my feelings of teenaged immortality, I went into this trip with the perspective that the world had finally opened up and that I was free.

We stayed at a little Casino; it was mesmerizing to me. My friend and I walked around in circles, watching the trapeze and acrobat act in one corner, puppets in another, games, lights, sounds, bells, smells, and so many people, all in one place. Eventually, we found our way outside and almost immediately we found people who could help us find what we were looking for. It wasn't long before we had found ourselves behind a building smoking, toking, and drinking with a few guys of varying ages. I vividly remember sitting on the edge of the concrete sidewalk next to my friend when we saw blue and red lights flashing. A cop car had stopped nearby.

Immediately after that, some officers stood right in front of us. Holding our beers between our legs, we were given a strong verbal warning to go about our business while minding our P's and Q's. They did dump out our beers though. Looking back on what would be thirty-seven years ago, I cannot see this situation unfolding the way it did back then in the present day. I think nowadays, those officers would not have asked nicely and all of us would have been on the ground in less than thirty seconds.

That little scare did nothing to slow me down and that was not how that day ended, unfortunately. I'm still not sure how that transition took place or what the hell *anyone* in that situation was thinking. After what seemed like only a few short minutes after the officers dumped out our beers, I was alone in a car with an older man, on the way to a hotel. I can't remember how old he was—thirty-five? Fifty? I remember that at first my mixed-up, confused, teenaged head was in a fog and that I was feeling no fear, just *excitement*, leaving with this man. Not long after, my head began to clear, and I felt a strong sense of shame. That shame cascaded into a sense of very low self-worth mixed with dread in anticipation of the act I knew so clearly was going to happen.

I made my way out of the hotel room afterwards. With a just a quick good-bye and a wave, I was back to walking along the unfamiliar streets of Reno. I was alone this time. Before a complete sense of panic took over, I spotted the familiar sight of the little-big Casino less than ten blocks away. Getting myself up to our room seemed like a feat more difficult than navigating an entire city full of bumper-to-bumper, shoulder-to-shoulder busyness. Once I got up there, I was greeted by my friend, sitting up on one of the beds. I truly wish I knew what she felt about my flightiness on our trip together. I can guess now that it was probably more than one emotion. That list likely contained feeling terrified that she had lost me to something dangerous and being livid that I had given her such a valid reason to worry.

Needless to say, like most of the situations I got myself into around this time, I was lucky to come out alive on the other side.

Back in my hometown, my friends and I would often sit at the train station, making fun of the tourists that came to visit our little town. We kept our jokes and comments to ourselves, privately laughing among ourselves. At the time, we could not fathom why anyone would want to come here, especially since the main attraction was a huge tree stump—very uninteresting in our opinions. That tree stump was actually an old-growth Douglas Fir log and is now sheltered in the middle of town. When we were not poking fun at tourists or hanging out by the river, we would walk around town. There were plenty of rivers, valleys, and abandoned logging trails to explore in our area. We would walk around for hours that turned into days, always seeking to settle our restless young souls.

This restlessness led us into some unexpected situations. There is no better example of this then the time a teen-carnie broke my collarbone. I was seventeen and another day turned into an evening while hanging out with the R.R's. That's what we called ourselves: 'R.R.s', the local kids who hung out on the banks of the river. That weekend, the local carnival and street fair was happening in our tiny town. The carnival workers had arrived earlier in the week and one teen worker befriended some of the R.R's. We stood around with our new acquaintance, talking and laughing while smoking and passing around a bottle of whiskey. All of the sudden, I hear, "Tag-team wrestling!" The carnie then picked me up faster than I could understand what was happening and flipped me onto my back. I hit the ground hard and knew in that quick moment that I was hurt. I tried to move but my shoulder felt like it was on fire.

Since this story happened in a time before everyone had a cellphone, my friends walked me a quarter mile to the nearest phone booth to call my mom. Wow, that sobered me up quick! My mom drove down the one main street into town to pick me up and taking me to our quaint local clinic to have me patched up. I remember telling mom, "Don't tell Daddy." I can laugh at myself when I recall that request—like he would never find out, funny girl. There were repercussions after this event, absolutely. Those stories, however, are not all mine to tell.

13

THE EDUCATION PROCESS

"Because post-traumatic symptoms are so persistent and so wide-ranging, they may be mistaken for enduring characteristics of the victim's personality. This is a costly error, for the person with unrecognized post-traumatic stress disorder is condemned to a diminished life, tormented by memory and bounded by helplessness and fear."[21]

As I prepared to enter high school, I remember feeling a similar optimism as to the start of seventh grade. I walked into freshman registration thinking that this was going to be my chance to change things. I even signed up for the drill team, cautiously excited for the chance to hangout and dance in choreographed unison with other freshman girls during football games. True to form, this optimism fizzled out as quickly as it ignited. I ended up avoiding drill team all together, unconsciously fearful to re-experience the awkward feelings of not-belonging. *It probably sucks anyways,* I thought.

This agitation and willingness to fight followed me through high school. By the end of my sophomore year, I had been in a few fights. Sometimes it was for personal reasons and other times it was requested. One time a friend asked me to fight a girl for him. My friend had mentioned that he had been slapped in the face by his girlfriend and couldn't do it himself. After school, I went to the local park where I knew she would be and beat

---

[21] Herman, *Trauma and Recovery,* 49.

the living shit out of her. Another time, in high school, I showed up at a boyfriend's house unannounced I knew his parents were out of town, so I let myself in and that's when I saw a girl's overnight bag on the couch. In a blur of rage, I stormed into his house where I found them, grabbed that girl by her hair, and dragged her out of the house. I was beating her senseless until my dickhead boyfriend pulled me off her. As he held my arms behind my back, the other girl kneed me in my nose. Since his parents were out of town and mine believed firmly in natural consequences, I had to deal with that injury on my own, leaving me with a crooked nose to this day.

When I was home, I usually kept to myself. I preferred to be home alone, wanting to avoid too much interaction with my family. Sometimes I did actually enjoy sitting on the couch watching TV with mom, observing dad's friends as they sat around the table telling jokes while smoking and drinking. Back then, mom and dad both smoked in the home. All the tables had ashtrays on them which was a normal thing at that time. In the summertime, mom and I would take down the panels off the ceiling and scrub them with bleach and wait for them to dry in the sun before hanging them back up.

When I did stay up in my room, I spent my time reading. My love for Stephen King's books started as I was ending middle school and I spent countless hours getting wrapped up in his stories. The collection of his books I started around this time continues to grow to this day. I had already developed a fondness for books about love in elementary school, so after every couple of King's books, I would treat myself to a romance novel. When I wasn't reading, I would listen to music or watch MTV. One of the things I did consistently was the daily act of changing my bedroom around. I would rearrange my drawers, reorganize my closets, and decorate and redecorate again and again.

I had become overly confrontational as a teen, often exploding over little things. When I tried to get my point across during an argument, I would get overwhelmed by the intensity of my emotions and cry uncontrollably. When I heard company come over to visit my parents, I would crank my music, listening to AC/DC, Ozzy Osbourne, Judas Priest, and Iron Maiden. Those 80's rockers were my idols. They embodied rebellion and their lyrics supported my world view. I would buy magazines that had pull-out posters of these bands and plaster my walls with them. That loud music with its strong bass and drums allowed me to drown out the rest of the world, if only for a little while.

My friends and I wore black t-shirts, miniskirts, holey pants with a black leather studded belts, and upside-down cross earrings that we had made. I wore my hair long and a bit spiky. Occasionally, we would use hydrogen peroxide to create bright streaks of yellowish white in our hair. This rebelliousness united us throughout our teen years, including our decision to leave that bullshit scene of high school all together.

My decision to drop out of high school happened about a week into my junior year. I had pulled up to my friend's house to pick her up for school like I did every morning. When I walked up to the door to let her know I had arrived, she opened it before my hand reached the doorknob. Excitedly, she told me that she had told her mom that we were no longer going to attend our high school. We had been talking about dropping out and this must be that day, I thought. So, I drove back home and told my mom the news. We were officially high-school drops-outs.

Although the rebellious side of me was thrilled to no longer be surrounded by the popular kids and authority figures, another part of me still wanted a diploma. It wasn't long after I dropped out before I enrolled in the local alternative high school. Their classes ran in the evening, making it easier for students to work during the day.

There were probably around thirty or so senior students in my class. Only about half of those made it to graduation. I was able to combine the classes I took in-person with mail-in correspondence classes which provided me with extra credit hours. With these extra credits, I was able to technically graduate a semester before the graduation ceremony. As I proudly walked on stage to accept my diploma, I knew that it was my tenacity (and a little bit of God's grace) that had allowed me to accomplish what I did. This memory, this sense of pride in my own autonomy, became one of those beautiful moments I treasure.

14

WORKING LIFE

"I learned the value of hard work from working hard."

-Margaret Mead

Throughout my life, I have always been a hard worker. I started babysitting for a few of my parent's friends when I was about eleven years old. It was not long after I started babysitting that I was asked by a few other families in town to help look after their kids too. Around the time I was thirteen, my mother worked at a local movie theater. I helped out there once or twice a week. I helped her clean up the trash left by movie-goers and then working with her at the concession stand. Mom would help me count back change for the theater's patrons. I remember feeling anxious about the responsibility of handling money but loved working with my mom. Occasionally, I would have the opportunity to see a movie there. The film that I most clearly remember seeing there around that time was *Star Wars: The Empire Strikes Back*. I saw that film as many times as I could before it left the theater and loved it every time.

The movie theater was ran by one of my mom's best friend's family. Their family had five kids and looking after them became one of my babysitting jobs. I remember sitting down with my mom before going to babysit. We would go through the TV Guide and mark the shows I could watch after putting the kids to bed. I felt very confident in my baby-sitting abilities. Not only did I look after the kids, but I also helped with chores around the house. I always made a point of not only cleaning up after myself and the kids, but I always made a point to wash all the dishes, clean off the counters, and tidied up the kids' bedrooms as well. My mom was always very supportive of me working and instilled in me a good work ethic. She encouraged me to go 'above and beyond' as a worker. I learned quickly that upholding this standard usually resulted in more money from appreciative employers. I liked making my own money, and tips were always a welcome bonus. I felt proud that I could go shopping for little things without asking my mom for money. I liked going to Pay-N-Save and Kmart to spend my earnings on new jewelry, records, and magazines.

When I was able to join the workforce at sixteen, I started working for my dad. I helped him out with asphalt and septic system jobs. Dad also taught me how to run a small backhoe. As a teen, I was primarily interested in money to pay for my telephone party line, gas for the car, new clothes, and the occasional bag of weed. At about sixteen or seventeen, I started working with my older brother as his apprentice, taping and mudding sheetrock. If any of my jobs as a young woman kept me in shape, it was this one. I could carry a full sheet, sometimes two, of sheetrock into houses for him. I could carry the mud to the designated mixing area then dump and mix the mud in the buckets. Honestly though, it really did build character. I was often the only female on a jobsite, and I pushed myself to be as self-sufficient as any of the guys. The work was often exhausting but overcoming the challenge proved to myself that I could do it.

I hated being the designated sander, but I did it when I had to. I do not believe I was especially helpful in this area. I had been told more than once that he had to mud over the places where I had sanded off all the mud, essentially re-doing the entire area himself. He would never hide my mistakes from me, however, and always took the time to show me how to do it better next time. He took pride in his work like our dad taught us and was good at what he did. His skills landed him some jobs at some incredibly ritzy places. I cannot even describe some of the homes we worked on. They were beyond anything I might have seen otherwise.

Around the time I was working with my big brother, I also was also cleaning rooms in the same town that would be the location of my next job. I started working at factory counting floppy disks, packaged them, then they were sent down the line. The work was dull, but I did meet some interesting people while working there.

One of my coworkers told me that she was a witch and shared some of her practices with me. Always a fascination of mine. As I continued to work there, I started to develop friendships and started to socialize with some people outside of work hours. Soon after, I began to date one of my coworkers. Our relationship was intimate, yet brief, as we both lost interest in dating after a few weeks. This romance was significant only by ways of introducing me to Abuser D.

Abuser D was a coworker, and we went on a few dates together. He didn't pressure me to be intimate. It was really refreshing to have no sexual expectations placed upon me at the beginning of a relationship. This allowed me to get to know this man who seemed reserved, caring, and kind. We held hands and the energy was not the sexually charged. He didn't talk a lot which allowed me to open up to him about some of the stuff that had happened to me. I talked to him about my history of abuse, hoping that he, unlike my past boyfriends, was someone I could trust.

15

CARETAKER

"When a person is completely powerless, and any form of resistance is futile, she may go into a state of surrender. The system of self-defense shuts down entirely. The helpless person escapes from her situation not by action in the real world but rather by altering her state of consciousness. Sometimes situations of inescapable danger may evoke not only terror and rage, but also, paradoxically, a state of detached calm, in which terror, rage, and pain dissolve. Events continue to register in awareness, but it is as though these events have been disconnected from their ordinary meanings. Perceptions may be numbed or distorted, with partial anesthesia or the loss of particular sensations. Time sense may be altered, often with a sense of slow motion, and the experience may lose its quality of ordinary reality. The person may feel as though the event is not happening to her, as though she is observing from outside her body, or as though the whole experience is a bad dream from which she will shortly awaken. These perceptual changes combine with a feeling of indifference, emotional detachment, and profound passivity in which the person relinquishes all initiative and struggle. This altered state of consciousness might be regarded as one of nature's small mercies, a protection against unbearable pain."[22]

It was not long after beginning my relationship with Abuser D that I was asked to be an assistant caretaker for a home on a little island, surrounded by great, gorgeous cliffs. The position was offered by an older gentleman, the caretaker, who Abuser D knew and to whom he had recommended me for the job. He was looking for someone who could provide some general upkeep, to mow the lawn and take care of the flowers around the outside of the house. The description of the land did not do it justice. The property included fifty-two acres of picturesque landscapes. There was an old-growth forest, natural water features, and a cliff on the far side of the property that provided amazing views of what was to be my future home. When I toured the property with the owner before accepting the job, I was swept up in its natural beauty. It seemed like a fairy-tale. When I excitedly told Abuser D about wanting to accept the job, he drove us out to the bridge that looked over the water. I could not have known that revisiting this same scenic vista many years later would inspire terror.

About a week had gone by living at the property. I had settled into the top loft in the caretaker's home, bringing some personal items as well as my two orange cats. One night, after finishing up the dishes in the kitchen, I walked into the living room to sit down with Abuser D and watch television. Before I was able to sit down, Abuser D rushed me. Before I knew what was happening, he had forced me to the ground and started to rape me. I remember that he kept slapping me—he wanted me to cry.[23] This is when I felt a shift deep within my core as darkness came surging forward to protect me. The last thing in the world I was going to do was to cry. My past experiences had taught me how to go numb, to disconnect from what was happening to my body. I let go of reality and waited for it to be over, my dry eyes stared unfixed off into the distance. No more memories were made that night in my dissociative state. I never saw Abuser D again after that night.

---

[22] Ibid, 42-43.

[23] "The purpose of the rapist is to terrorize, dominate, and humiliate his victim, to render her utterly helpless. Thus rape, by its nature, is intentionally designed to produce psychological trauma." Ibid., 58.

The next day, I was able to get to a phone and call my mom. She and my older brother rushed over to pick me up. She talked me through what items I needed to pack for her to take me home. I remember her explaining that she would arrange for the rest of my things and, of course, my cats to be brought back later. We had to go. Now.

I don't remember looking back or what I was thinking other than that this story-book home had come to be just another scene in my on-going nightmare. The car ride home was silent, and my assault was never talked about again. Later I was told that he took himself somewhere to 'get help.' *What the hell did that mean?* That man escaped consequences as well—just like the other abusers. It sounded to me like his violent actions were being swept under the rug, like what seemed to always happen. Once again, I was waving frantically from behind a window. Surely, *now* I would receive justice. *Now* my attacker would be punished and be forced to face what he did to me, right? My hopeful plea was met with silence.

16

NOT REAL LOVE

"While human contact and attunement are the wellspring of physiological self-regulation, the promise of closeness often evoke fear of getting hurt, betrayed, and abandoned. Shame plays an important role in this: "You will find out how rotten and disgusting I am and dump me as soon as you really get to know me." Unresolved trauma can take a terrible toll on relationships. If your heart is still broken because you were assaulted by someone you loved, you are likely to be preoccupied with not getting hurt again and fear opening up to someone new. If fact, you may unwittingly try to hurt them before they have a chance to hurt you."[24]

After returning home, I continued to work and the depression I had been fighting off since childhood deepened and my insomnia grew stronger. My mind attempted to make sense of the repeated sexual assaults I had experienced. My beliefs were altered to fit within a cruel reality. I began to believe that I did not deserve to be treated with kindness or respect. This meant that the relationships I would form would always be abusive in one way or the other. I just had to accept that fact and move on. I even took back that dickhead who helped that girl break my nose. To protect my heart, I treated my body carelessly. If I didn't respect my sexuality, then it didn't matter if no one else

---

[24] Van Der Kolk, *The Body Keeps the Score*, 211.

did either[25]. I used my sexual promiscuity as a young woman to control what I could of my sexual narrative. I tried to embody that horrifyingly toxic phrase, 'You can't rape the willing,' in too many situations. I involved myself in many relationships, dating boys or young men, during childhood and my young adult years. Eventually, I appreciated the long-term relationships, feeling truly cared for, versus the hurtful, unhealthy, emotionally and physically painful.

Still filling the emotional void with drugs, my use becoming more varied and frequent after high school. After graduation, I went to laser light shows on psychedelic mushrooms. I then experimented with acid a couple of times and hated it. I had my fair share of crank and barely survived the series of events that followed that drug choice. I had also started smoking cocaine around this time. I remember how I would make trips out of town, *way* out of town, to get drugs for half-price. The plan had been to make some money by selling the stuff back in town. Unsurprisingly, the product was always consumed before that happened.

So much about reality was warped by being high. One blurry evening, I left a party house about twenty miles outside town to go home. I ended up passing my house by a least sixty miles. Once I realized what I had done, I quickly called home to get directions back. Remember, this was a time before cellphones and GPS navigation. Sometime after this, I remember being in a car with a friend, driving through a busted part of a different town. We were rear ended while I was throwing a line on a mirror. That was not the last time the potential for police involvement was a bit too close for comfort. In the same town on a different night, I left a friends' house around three in the morning. I was just a couple of blocks down the road when I made a 'free left' turn in front of a cop. Luckily, the officer was part of my community and recognized my last name, so I was let off with a warning.

My years of drug use wrapped up one night when I was sitting up in the trails a few miles from home, smoking crack until my heart felt like it was going to beat itself out of my chest. I somehow managed to drive myself home and get into bed around one. I was sure that my body was telling me that I crossed a line. I thought for sure that my chest was going to explode.

---

[25] "The risk of rape, sexual harassment, or battering, though high for all women, is approximately doubled for survivors of childhood sexual abuse." Herman, *Trauma and Recovery*, 111.

While I was lying in bed, willing my heart to stay within my ribcage, all I could think about was how disappointed, sad, and angry my parents were going to be if I had to go wake them up and ask them to take me to the hospital because I just overdosed. I prayed, held my chest tight, and prayed some more. That was one of the most awful, unforgettable nights of my life.

I was working with my brother at this point in my life and he and his wife invited me to live with them. They had just moved there and the drive to work was much shorter from his house, so it made sense. At this time, I had begun to date a young man who was introduced to me as a journeyman sheet-rocker from work. Being closer to him was also part of my motivation for moving into my big brother's home. For the sake of other's privacy and to make a long story short, we dated for about a year before I graduated high school. Our relationship was less than healthy. I just did not get it yet that it could be better. I was still unaware that I had the ability to be in a relationship where I didn't have to beg to be loved instead of used. Most importantly, I had not realized that this sort of pain was unnecessary to endure. I still thought I deserved to suffer in order to be loved.

When I was turning nineteen, I started to date a man that I would marry, decades later. I attended a local bonfire one evening and was introduced to a new guy in the neighborhood by a couple of friends. We were quick to become 'comfortable' with each other after meeting. We then dated for a couple of years before meeting back up again years later.

I, like many others, could fill volumes of stories of drama and heartache. Looking back, I can see how confused I was about what a relationship was at this time. I have also reflected on my lack of healthy emotional and relational skills contributed to said drama and heartache. I swam toward the familiarity of hurt and turmoil. I yearned to be comforted, accepted, and nurtured, but did not understand how to accept those acts of love for myself yet. The frustration I felt at being unable to fulfill my emotional needs started the cycle of attacking or refusing the love I so desperately wanted, only to grieve the loss when I succeeded in pushing it away.[26]

---

[26] "The survivor's intimate relationships are driven by the hunger for protection and care and are haunted by the fear of abandonment or exploitation. [...] Ordinary interpersonal conflicts may provoke intense anxiety, depression, or rage. [...] Thus the survivor develops a pattern of intense, unstable relationships, repeatedly enacting dramas of rescue, injustice, and betrayal." Ibid., 111.

17

LOVE AND LABOR

"Courage is not having the strength to go on; it is going on when you don't have the strength."

– Theodore Roosevelt

I kept busy after graduation. At nineteen, I was signed up for the Labor Union out of Seattle. Being a part of the Union led to an experience of a lifetime. I dug ditches, flagged traffic, laid pipe, and became proficient in using a rivet buster (a small jack hammer) to break up lagging walls that held back soil like a dam does water. I worked alongside drillers, carpenters, and the heavy equipment operators, all the other laborers. I ended up having to return to Kingston for my laborer's training. There, I completed my hazmat and asbestos removal certifications.

With those certifications, I later had the opportunity to work on cleaning up an oil spill in Tacoma. This job was done in a full Tyvek suit and entailed going through a decontamination station on our way back from the spill in order to not spread the oily mess. I worked the swing shift and that was perfect for me. I was able to enjoy my night owl lifestyle, staying up to read or engage in whatever hobby I wanted to at the time, often while watching some scary movie or TV show. The other side of the swing shift was having an actual part of the weekday to do any shopping or errands that couldn't be done on the weekends. Before having kids, night and swing shifts had always been my preference.

On another job, I worked on a bridge as a flagger and laborer. There I worked with concrete trucks and road-stripers. It was this job where I met my first husband. He was the heavy equipment operator on the job, running cranes, track hoes, and other equipment. I was often his flagger or laborer. One day at work, I had been asked to go to a bar by another man on the job and actually asked my future first husband to be our chaperone. After that, we got together and started dating with our marriage following not too far behind.

Working as a flagger for union contractors provided a whole other level of skills and opportunities. Once I was assigned to flag for a road crew, located on the road up to the mountain base. This position entailed that I flag cars traveling on the road to stop when the crew was working. Flaggers took turns driving the pilot truck and standing on the road with our signs. Occasionally, the road would get busy and there would be lines of twenty or more stopped cars. Usually, the road was not as busy and my job kept me along the same route, so I began to recognize faces on their commutes as the days went by. No one was ever thrilled about being delayed, but some people took advantage of the pause to chat with me. I eventually looked forward to talking to some of the regular commuters.

As I continued to train and grow my laborer skills, I was placed in a position at a large Dam as a stress-tester, helping to ensure that the structure could withstand the incredible weight and pressure. I learned how to work with the grade checkers and welders on site, knowing that everyone's safety relied on total workplace cooperation. At least once per day the warning horns would sound, signaling to us that a detonation blast was imminent. Workers would crawl out of whatever crevice they were in and then quickly scramble to get to safety. I remember ducking behind the job shacks with my coworkers, listening for the shower of rocks and boulders to hit the other side. Working in the mines at the dam was interesting, scary, and short-lived. I'm sure I worked there for less than two weeks before the job was complete, and I moved on to the next one.

Building my skills as a laborer was very empowering for me as a young woman. I was grateful that I had the opportunity to learn skills that not many other females I knew sought to develop. It was also gratifying to know that my efforts contributed to the completion of some impressive jobs and projects. While working as a laborer, I learned that I could do more than what most people expected from me. Although my statue was small, I was strong and able to competently do hard work. In fact, I preferred to work as a laborer opposed to a flagger because a laborer's job was more physically demanding. I built up mental toughness as well. There were more times than I could count when my presence on a work site inspired catcalls or other unwelcome commentary. I learned to let these roll off my back by ignoring them all together and depriving whoever was making them the satisfaction of any reaction. I continued to work on construction jobs until I was about six months pregnant with my son. I remember that while I was pregnant and working on the job, finding consistent restroom access was a challenge. There were many times that I would hastily wave down a fellow laborer to cover for me so I could find a semi-private patch of trees, struggle to pull down my Carhart overalls over my growing belly, and squat.

My satisfaction in my job was nourished by my parents' pride in my skills. Whenever someone would complement my work or when I was offered a desirable job, I always looked forward to telling my parents about it. My daddy was so proud, always telling people how I was, "kicking ass and taking names!" and "She's one of the best laborers on the job!" Obviously, my dad may have been a bit biased toward his girl, but I always glowed at his praise. I appreciated hearing that they were proud of me, but I valued their advice perhaps more so. Since they had always been hard workers, they were able to advise me in polishing my job performance and offering other tips and tricks when they were relevant for me. I was conscientious of not allowing my gender to be used as a base of favoritism or discrimination. I worked hard and carried my own weight, no matter what. Incorporating my parents' work ethic into my own has helped carry me through a lifetime of employment.

18

MOTHERHOOD

"Many survivors are terribly afraid that their children will suffer a fate similar to their own, and they go to great lengths to prevent this from happening. For the sake of their children, survivors are often able to mobilize caring and protective capacities that they have never been able to extend to themselves."[27]

I can look back and see many beautiful moments. I can see the time I spent with my parents as a child, our special moments of connection. I can see my initiative in my schooling and work. An especially empowering memory was when I opened my own licensed childcare and preschool programs. The responsibility of providing the quality care that all children deserve inspired me to stay current on early childhood development and education research. I was constantly learning new things and honing my skills.

My career in childcare began when my son was about six months old. Having a mom who provided childcare in our home growing up, I had absolutely established some expectations and standards when I went looking for childcare for my son. My opinions may be biased, but the childcare program I saw my mother run was high-quality and compassionately provided for the needs of every kiddo who was entrusted to her care. After looking at many childcare providers and program in the area, I knew that I wouldn't leave a stray dog in the care of some of the places I visited and

---

[27] Ibid., 114.

would absolutely not trust them to care for my infant son. After seeing how poor the childcare system was in my area, I decided that I would have to be the one to provide the quality of childcare that I knew my son, and all kids, deserved. So that is when I started to gather my resources and started making a plan to become a licensed childcare provider and owner.

There have been so many people who have shared their joys and hardships with me among the families I have worked with and cared for. Many of the friendships I have made have been lifelong, whether they were coworkers or clients. I loved the work and most importantly to me, I was now in a position where I could advocate or help the children in my care when I saw the need. Due to my own trauma history, I was quick to recognize behaviors and signs indicating abuse when I saw them. I learned to monitor my feelings to avoid becoming triggered and overly angry when I suspected someone had hurt one of my kiddos. I also learned that being a mandated reported did not mean being a mandated investigator. My job was to report and allow for the investigation to proceed, which was something beyond my professional abilities.

Being able to be home with my two babies was greater than any job I could have taken. As a licensed childcare provider, I was offered full academic scholarships in order to further my knowledge and education. I took advantage of this scholarship and earned my degree during this time. Unfortunately, my bachelor's degree was not covered by scholarships, and I now have some hellish student loan bills.

I took my job and my education very seriously and emphasized providing a safe and enriching environment for the kiddos. I always have been proud that I was able to open a childcare program and have my roster full within a few months. I took in as many toddlers and preschoolers as I could legally fit. I learned the States Codes that maintained the standards of quality childcare. I have always been amazed at some people's understanding of what 'quality childcare' meant, especially thinking back to the places that inspired (*horrified*) me to open my own program. My in-home programs always included preschool and fieldtrips. We would go to nearby parks, the zoo, the children's museum, and the state capitol buildings to name a few. When I look back at my ability and willingness to take all those little ones on trips or on whatever errands I hauled us all to that day, I can appreciate all those times. Currently, I don't care much to go to the store alone or if it's not necessary.

Continuing to work in the childcare field as my own children grew into their teen years was a whole other adventure. As you might be able to imagine, there were both pros and cons of parenting teens while caring for groups of little ones, but I still would not have changed a thing. Unfortunately, it was around this time that my first husband and I were separating, and in the process, we lost the home that we had purchased with the money I inherited after my mother passed. Our home was also my place of work. It was a hard decision after thirteen years to close the business I had poured so much of myself into. For a time after I closed the program, I was a nanny for a couple of daycare kids that I had been looking after since they were two years old. I then had an opportunity to be a Head Start teacher for a while. After that, I transitioned into a program supervisor position for large childcare center that included preschool along with childcare, which seemed a lot like what I used to do, on a much larger scale. The opportunity to work with so many kids and families seemed challenging, but in a good way. I knew that there I would have the chance to do good for a lot of kiddos, and that was reason enough.

19

THE CENTER

"Any system that values profit over human life is a very dangerous one indeed."

— Suzy Kassem

I landed at the childcare center toward the end of my career. The center had up to twenty-four employees who looked after about 127 kiddos, on average. I was a working program supervisor which meant that I was on the floor working, observing, or training teachers. The program's director was extremely knowledgeable and had ran her own in-home childcare program just as I had. Understandably, we shared a lot of the same ideals for how quality care should be provided. Despite our similarities, we had two completely different ways of getting things done. We turned this difference into a strength, however, particularly when it came to addressing problems with staff. I took on the role of going to the staff members to communicate issues or work through problems. We decided this was best since when she tried to address issues with staff, they ended up upset and crying or worse, becoming angry and then quitting. When that happened, the whole system at the center was strained as it tried to compensate for an unexpected vacancy in staffing. So, we definitely did not want that happening, if possible. While I handled most of the communication with staff, she shared her knowledge and a great many lessons with me. She also provided me opportunities to learn what *not* to do in situations as well, which was just as valuable.

Throughout my time working at the center, I was truly committed to the program and was proud of the team that was being created there. The director was confident in my ability to manage the center if she was not there. My supports in the office and a handful of amazing teachers made the job seem very easy some days. I was proud that I could walk into any of the rooms and watch kids of all different ages learning and growing. When I visited the classrooms, the kiddos would excitedly greet me and immediately want to show me something, sing me a song they learned, or just sit and talk while creating or playing with a favorite toy. I was happy and proud to be a part of this experience for them and be a positive part of so children and their families' lives.

My position at the center unexpectedly changed one day after I returned from a rare lunch outing. When I got back to the center, things were tense, and my director appeared to be upset. She had been crying and did not want to talk. I am not able to provide details to what happened, but the conclusion of the situation was that I was to step into the role of director the following morning. Even though I had years of professional childcare experience, I felt intimidated by the position. I was humbled by so many staff member's support and encouragement and humbled by the faith of those around me who believed I could do it. So, the next day, I transitioned from my work on the Early Achievers resources to taking up the mantle of director.

I was not always as confident as my peers and coworkers were in my abilities, but my heart was always there. I believed in being passionate about what you loved to do and being compassionate to those around us and wanted to emphasize this in my role as a leader. I must again give credit to an amazing team. Everyone in the office, classrooms, and the kitchen were a key part of making it all happen. I cannot express enough gratitude for their support and teamwork. As the director, I worked long hours. I felt the obligation to each and every child and their families to provide them the best childcare environment that could be offered. I did my best to model good work ethic for my team members. It was important to me to that we each did our job as best as we could.

The owner of the center developed some serious medical issues which left him unable to properly attend to his responsibilities as a business owner. His adult children had the idea that they were going to attempt to keep the center running if it were profitable. Otherwise, they planned to sell. Unfortunately for the center, they had absolutely no idea how to run a childcare center while still providing quality care for the children that were in it. At this point, I had been in this field for thirty years and had a lot of experience regarding the ownership and operation of a childcare business, and I saw some major issues that needed to be addressed if the center were to stay open. I was aware that the rent for the building was outrageously high and as the new owners made changes to the program, I saw that very few that were in the kids' best interest.

Accepting that things were changing and not for the better, I knew that I needed to prepare to move on. I started to talk to potential directors, looking for someone qualified to take my place. I had just hired a young, skilled program supervisor who also worked well with the teachers and families. She could have potential. At this time, I was also preparing to marry my second husband. We lived over 500 miles apart, so the commute was substantial. For ten months, I drove just under five hours, one-way, because I was so concerned about leaving the center without a good director.

One day, I held an interview with an unscheduled walk-in. It was not common to have walk-in applicants, but I decided to be flexible that day since my schedule allowed for it. When the new owners found out that I had held an interview without them being present, they were furious. Tensions had been mounting between us for a while at that point. I had outright refused to understaff the center to save money like they had wanted. The adult-child ratios outlined by the state exist for a reason and I would not allow for my or any staff to risk the integrity of their license by not meeting the standards set within the administrative codes. This was the final straw for them. After berating me, they told me to leave.

The end of my time at the center was devastating. My dedication, the years building a great team, the pride of knowing that I helped create a place that was truly *good,* was crushed in less than a minute. The hurt did not end at my termination. I felt betrayed by the staff who said nothing to defend me. I felt betrayed again when I learned that the program supervisor I had recruited had stepped into the role of director. It soured my stomach to know that the new owners had placed someone so green into this role to save on time and effort, never mind the fact that she was not qualified.

I learned that some staff members did decide to demonstrate their disapproval about my termination. One staff member, who is still dear to my heart, quit immediately in solidarity. About a half dozen more had been watching the center crumble under the new owners, this was an out. They told me that they had been treated awful. They told me that I was the only person who cared enough to keep everyone safe and the standards for care high, not just lip service. From what I heard about the center's fate after I left, they reduced the teacher's salaries, leading to even more people walking out. The center quickly started to lose families faster than they could attract new ones. Needless to say, when I heard that they had ended up going under, I wasn't sad.

I was in mourning for my old life where I knew the job that I was doing mattered and having that purpose validated by the happiness of the kids and families I worked with. I began to sink into a deep depression, feeling suffocated by the void of where my career in childcare use to be. I decided that a fresh start in a new state could be good for me. I wanted nothing more than to be where I was, in my new home, with my husband.

The dramatic transition from my last year at the daycare center to my new home and getting married, left me with bittersweet emotions. I was excited to start my life with my new husband and not caring for the distance between me and my adult children. I was also not feeling very comfortable about leaving my, less then healthy dad behind.

I exchanged my thirty-year career in childcare for the position of 'bookkeeper' for my husband's business. That job title ended up including the roles of office coordinator and account as well—not my areas of expertise. Quickly realizing that this bookkeeper gig was not going to pan out, I decided I needed to look elsewhere for work that supported my self-worth.

20

AN UNEXPECTED LOSS

"Life need not be long-lived for it to be meaningful."

-Unknown

My passion for caring for children was in part inspired by my mother, partly my own love of little ones, and partly due the experience of loss. A part of my transition into parenthood was coming to understand the heartache that can come with that much love. Shortly after moving in with my first husband, before we were officially married, I had a miscarriage. I was working as a laborer on a job site, having what I thought was one of the worst periods of my life. I could hardly stand up straight and felt like I just needed to go to the bathroom or something at first. I left work early and ended up in the hospital that night. After I was admitted, I was told that I was having a miscarriage and then a flurry of activity followed, preparing for whatever was to happen next. It was so unexpected. I was surprised and so excited to be pregnant at the same time of being indescribably sad at the loss of the baby on top of being in so much pain. I felt like it broke me. At one point, I told the nurse that I needed to use the bedpan. The next thing I saw was my baby's lifeless little body in that bedpan I asked for. I will always carry that image with me.

The nurse asked if she could pray with me. This was one of those memorable moments of one human demonstrating to another sincere compassion with no expectations of anything in return. We didn't really even know each other but that didn't matter to either of us. I know that she went above and beyond her job's responsibilities in that moment and I will always be grateful for her kindness.

My emotions went numb, I was a zombie person for a couple of weeks after that. I couldn't breathe when my thoughts drifted back to that day. Guilt-heavy questions constantly bombarded my mind. *How did I not know? I was on pain meds recently after hurting your back—did that do it? Or was it when I picked up the gang-box that hurt my back in the first place? There was lead paint being removed from the jobsite—was that why I lost the baby? Is it just not the right time, like everyone keeps saying?* I will never know why I lost the baby but I will never forget the intensity of the love and grief I experienced over a child I was only aware of after they were already gone.

I eventually recovered from my grief and went on to give birth to the loves of my life, my 2 children. Motherhood has brought an incredible amount of purpose and meaning into my life and is a constant inspiration for working hard in my field. It has also led me to discover a whole new kind of strength that I had, a type of power that only a mother can understand.

The last empowering collection of moments I'll share here were my involvement in a Leadership Academy. This Leadership Academy was a group of people that provided unconditional quality childcare. Every second I spent improving the quality of care I provided, was worth it for those kids. My childcare experience and education have helped adults too. Whenever another childcare provider, friend, or family member asked for my advice about children, I felt a sense of pride and belonging. I knew that my advice could help them keep their kids safe, supported, and healthy.

21

DREAMS

"Just as traumatic memories are unlike ordinary memories, traumatic dreams are unlike ordinary dreams. In form, these dreams share many of the unusual features of the traumatic memories that occur in waking states. They often include fragments of the traumatic event in exact form, with little or no imaginative elaboration. Identical dreams often occur repeatedly. They are often experienced with terrifying immediacy, as if occurring in the present. Small, seemingly insignificant environmental stimuli occurring during these dreams can be perceived as signals of a hostile attack, arousing violent reactions. And the traumatic nightmares can occur in stages of sleep in which people do not ordinarily dream. Thus, in sleep as well as in waking life, traumatic memories appear to be based in an altered neurophysiological organization."[28]

My dreams have always been other-worldly. The surrealistic themes wove together people and places I knew, and some places I knew *not* to go. I learned how to fly in my dreams, how to jump and soar. That was my superpower there. I could fly over my town, looking down on the people I could see but could not see me. As with many trauma survivors, many of my dreams were reoccurring. I revisited the same places over and over, eventually learning more about them. I learned about the specifics of the

---

[28] Ibid., 39.

buildings, which doors I could or could not go through. Eventually, I taught myself how to escape these places as well. When I found myself in burning boxes or inside a little room from which I could not escape, I would start to sing the hymns I learned in Sunday school. When I started to sing, I would wake up. I later came to appreciate my vivid dreams—the ones that weren't nightmares. I would dream about being in the car with my mom, talking to her as we drove. When I could see her, I would reach out. Sometimes, I could hold her hand. Other times, I woke up before I could touch her.

I have had reoccurring dreams for as long as I can remember. Most were scary and I would wake up sad. The ones where I was buried caused panic attacks and I would jolt awake gripped with terror, my heart pounding. After those kinds of dreams, I stressed about how I was ever going to be able go back to sleep. I would try so hard to avoid the feelings of panic and fear of death that followed me to my waking state. Sometimes when I woke, I felt guilty and my thoughts turned to feelings that I was inherently bad. I tried to fight against these thoughts, but they were so strong.

In those long, tense nights, I would try not to think about how what happened after we die. Would I wake up from death like I wake up from dreams, trapped in a box underground? What if death is just closing our eyes and then we stop existing? I was afraid that God was going to punish me for my badness. I was taught that only a small amount of people go to heaven. I wanted to be one of those select few, of course, but as I lied there in the dark, I saw all these reasons why I shouldn't. My mind would list all my flaws, all my mistakes—all my shame laid out before me. During those nights when I would try to sooth myself from the terror inflicted on me by my nightmares, I felt trapped in my own hell and could see no reason why I did not belong there.

SOME FEELINGS OF DEPRESSION

I hope you NEVER feel uncomfortable
I hope you NEVER feel anxious
I hope you NEVER feel insecure
I hope you NEVER feel like you're not good enough
I hope you NEVER have to chase empathy from the one you love the most
I hope you NEVER feel like your mind just won't stop!!!
I hope you NEVER feel you are a burden
I hope you NEVER feel too afraid to speak your mind or express feelings
I hope you NEVER feel like you're alone in a room full of laughter
I hope you NEVER feel you have to fake a smile
I hope you NEVER feel disrespected
I hope you NEVER feel like a disappointment to others

I hope you NEVER feel like you wish you could just sleep and not wake up!

R. Nichols

"Those damaging thoughts I have about who I am, doesn't need to be. That is no longer who I am. I know more today than I did yesterday. I will know tomorrow more than I know today."

R. Nichols

22

GETTING HELP

"As survivors recognize and 'let go' of those aspects of themselves that were formed by the traumatic environment, they also become more forgiving of themselves. They are more willing to acknowledge the damage done to their character when they no longer feel that such damage must be permanent. The more actively survivors are able to engage in rebuilding their lives, the more generous and accepting they can be toward the memory of the traumatized self."[29]

I have been struggling to heal from being sexually assaulted since I can remember. Shortly after I turned sixteen, I made my first therapy appointment. I drove myself to it and then back again for a few more sessions. I remember that going to therapy felt very strange and that I had no idea what to expect. My first therapist specialized in hypnotherapy. I was not a hard believer in hypnosis, so while I appreciated the effort, the technique didn't feel like a good fit and I stopped going.

I told my mom that I was going to therapy after my first couple of sessions. My parents were not opposed to me going but could not understand what I expected to get out of it. They never discouraged me from seeking out mental health support. I think it was just something they did not know much about. The stigma of going to therapy was pretty strong in the 1980's and I assume they did not feel that outside help was

---

[29] Ibid., 203-204.

needed. My dad was transparent about a story about his own trauma and that he 'didn't need to get professional help about it' and that he was 'fine.' I have always understood that this is how many people feel. I also might beg-to-differ about the 'I'm fine' part that people like to express.

I went to different therapists, inconsistently, throughout the years. It was a few years into my first marriage when I started feeling the past sneaking up, its presence growing steadily heavier in my mind. This was also around the time that I had hired that detective to locate Abuser B. So again, I decided to seek out help in shaking off that heaviness. I found a therapist that lived only a couple miles away from my home. They also allowed me to trade some of my landscaping services in exchange for covering session fees. As therapy went on and we began to process through some of my traumatic experiences, I started to become triggered in sessions. The fear and pain in those memories were intense and recalling them pushed my nervous system into a fight-flight-or-freeze response. This experience is not uncommon when working through trauma but since I had no real mental health support outside of therapy sessions, I was not able to process the memories effectively or safely on my own. My newly exposed feelings felt dangerous, threatening to destroy the semblance of emotional stability I had fought so hard to create. So, I stopped going for a few years.

Throughout my time in therapy, I experienced short spurts of empowerment. It felt good to take care of myself in a positive way, even if I was not completely sure what *exactly* therapy was doing for me. I did not know at this time that to conquer the evil in the past, I had to accept it in its entirety first. After a while, I recognized that it really did help me when I processed through the painful memories in a safe space. When I talked about them, it helped me consolidate those ugly moments. The painful, fractured memories became more organized and less frightening. It was still difficult a lot of the time. When I would spiral into negative self-talk and began to express my desire to make all the dark thoughts and feelings *just stop*, it was like my head was slipping beneath the water. Following an intense experience in therapy, I agreed to sign a suicide prevention contract. I wondered out-loud about how that contract would hold up if I chose to act upon the ugly thoughts. I was asked to intentionally think about family and friends who I could reach out to for support. I appreciated being held accountable. At that time, this was enough to keep my head above water, figuratively and literally.

As I have gone through years of therapy, the work paid off. My mind is clearer, and my heart is not as heavy. The heaviness of each ugly event, the weight of feeling responsible for the abuse, and the pressure of feeling I had to be quiet about all of it, is absent most days. The best therapists I've worked with were sincere with their support and provided me with a safe, nonjudgmental space when I needed verbal and emotional outlets. Therapy helped me to recognize that I *was* doing something before learning about *why* I was doing something. I needed to see myself clearly before I could be seen by others. I needed to understand who I am to make the changes that I needed to heal. Therapy requires work, but that never intimidated me. I've always been a hard worker. I did the work that therapy required of me and am proud of what I have achieved. I've reached a place where giving up is finally not an option.

Staying away from diagnostic labels for me has been beneficial in managing the stigma of mental health issues yet knowing precisely *which* issue to treat makes finding the right tools or coping skill less challenging. I have been given the diagnoses of complex post-traumatic stress disorder (PTSD), major depressive disorder, and bipolar disorder with ongoing symptoms of obsessive-compulsive disorder. I have engaged in trauma-focused exposure therapy, systemic trauma therapy, neurofeedback therapy, and EMDR while writing this book.

Trauma-focused exposure therapy is designed to reduce symptoms of PTSD as well as helping to reduce accompanying issues like anger, guilt, and depression. Exposure therapy includes psychoeducation (learning about how trauma affects the biology of the brain), in vivo exposure (where someone gradually increases their exposure to a feared object or situation), imaginal exposure (where someone like me could re-visit memories of trauma with the therapist's supportive presence), and emotional processing—which is pretty much what it sounds like.[30]

Systemic trauma therapy includes standard trauma-related therapeutic interventions but also emphasizes the greater context in which the trauma

---

[30] Sheila A. Rauch, Afsoon Eftekhari, and Josef I. Ruzek, "Review of Exposure Therapy: A Gold Standard for PTSD Treatment," *The Journal of Rehabilitation Research and Development* 49, no. 5 (2012): pp. 679-688.

occurred. This means that while it is important to decrease trauma symptoms, it is just as important to address the ways our society, culture, and institutions give rise to trauma and impact our responses to traumatic disclosure.[31]

Neurofeedback is a type of therapy that provides moment-to-moment feedback of someone's physiological functioning with the help of machines that monitor the brain's electric signals. The feedback from the signals tells the patient about their central nervous system activation such as heart and respiratory rates, so the patient can then practice self-regulation when triggered. This process is used to teach the patient about emotional control while at the same time creating a deeper understanding of the impact of their emotions on their physical state.[32] At first, the experience was a bit overwhelming. My therapist helped me understand and lessen this feeling by explaining how the experience was a bit like going to a waterpark and standing at the top where all the slides start. The feeling I was having was my perceived need to attempt to go down all the slides at the same time. By focusing on just one or two slides at a time, I can take the pressure off of myself to do everything at once. Neurofeedback helped relieve some of the burden of my trauma. I felt as though it freed up space in my head for processing my past. I felt refreshed and able to focus. It was by no means a cure-all, but the timing of neurofeedback coming into my life was definitely a positive part of my therapeutic journey.

Eye Movement Desensitization and Reprocessing (EMDR) is a structured form of therapy that encourages the recipient to briefly focus on the traumatic memory while simultaneously experiencing bilateral stimulation (typically eye movements), which is associated with a reduction in the vividness and emotional intensity connected to the trauma

---

[31] Rachel E. Goldsmith, Christina Gamache Martin, and Carly Parnitzke Smith, "Systemic Trauma," *Journal of Trauma & Dissociation* 15, no. 2 (November 2014): pp. 117-132.
[32] Toshinori Chiba et al., "Current Status of Neurofeedback for Post-Traumatic Stress Disorder: A Systematic Review and the Possibility of Decoded Neurofeedback," *Frontiers in Human Neuroscience* 13 (2019), https://doi.org/10.3389/fnhum.2019.00233.

memories.[33] When it was explained to me how it worked, I understood that we would be going over one event at a time. I knew it would be hard, but I didn't know exactly *how* hard it would be until I was knee-deep in it. The process started with a couple of preparation sessions that included an extensive personality test and standard psychotherapy. When I first started the EMDR part, I was asked to rate from one to ten how horrible did the worst memory with Abuser A felt to me. Well, that's easy—*at least* twelve. To begin the reprocessing part, my therapist then held up two fingers and moved her hand side to side. I was instructed to focus and follow the movement with my eyes. After the first session, I rated that same memory as about a seven. At the start of the second session, it was still around a seven or six. With the therapist's support and more work on my part, it came down to about four. Going into my third session, I remember being concerned that I barely made it through the trauma with Abuser A and felt discouraged that I still had so far to go. I kept with it though and did the work.

My mind had revisited these painful memories before EMDR, of course, but reprocessing allowed me to alter my perception of them. I started to feel more connected to the present time, and while the memories were awful, they are just memories. I was no longer there. I was safe now and stronger than I have ever been. I was a survivor. My therapist encouraged me to conceptualize myself in parts: the vulnerable child, the protector/warrior, the nurturing mother, etc. Partway through the second session, I could vividly feel my tween self (my badass protector part) walking the five-year-old self down this hall and protecting her. I began to see more clearly the aspects of the memories of how I had tried to get away, of how I resisted. Almost immediately, I began to feel a sense of reclaiming some of my autonomy. Over time, I would take back that which was stolen from me: my innocent vulnerability, my sense of safety and trust, and my confidence that I could protect myself. Through a combination of my therapist's professional skills and my hard work and perseverance with the therapy, the rating ended up dropping to a two. At that point, I was ready to move onto what was next.

---

[33] "Eye Movement Desensitization and Reprocessing (EMDR) Therapy," American Psychological Association (American Psychological Association), accessed April 30, 2021, https://www.apa.org/ptsd-guideline/treatments/eye-movement-reprocessing.

These therapies have helped me work through difficult emotions instead of avoiding them and pushing them aside. Much of my hesitation in completing this book has been rooted in the fear of how others will respond. I have to remind myself, as I have been reminded by others, that this is my story, my reality, *my life*. Writing this book has been an act of self-love.

23

FULL CIRCLE

"Resolution of the trauma is never final; recovery is never complete. The impact of a traumatic event continues to reverberate throughout the survivor's lifecycle. Issues that were sufficiently resolved at one stage of recovery may be reawakened as the survivor reaches new milestones in her development. Marriage or divorce, a birth or death in the family, illness or retirement, are frequent occasions for a resurgence of traumatic memories."[34]

I was unable to avoid my attackers' presence forever. In my forties, my dad passed. I attended the service with my husband and on our drive in, I lost it. I didn't want to go and told him to keep driving once we got close. I think that, in my grief, I thought that if I didn't go to the funeral, the reality of my dad not being there would go away. After taking a little time to collect myself, I accepted what I was there to do. We arrived at the service.

There were many family members, friends, and neighbors in attendance. The turnout for each of my parents' funerals were tremendous, standing room only, showing how deeply beloved by so many they both were. I read the eulogy I had written and part of a letter that he had written to me in preschool while he was working in Alaska. I loved this letter. In it, he expressed his love for his whole family: me, both of my brothers, and mom. I truly believe that this love was not limited by having a physical

---

[34] Herman, *Trauma and Recovery,* 211.

body. Right after he passed, I saw the biggest, fluffiest white clouds join the beautiful, colorful sky and I knew that my parents were together again. My younger brother made a video of dad that he shared for the service as well. After my brother and I had our turns to speak, dad's friends were given the opportunity to share their own stories. I remember feeling so much love contained in their stories and felt their appreciation for my dad's presence in their lives.

The emotional rollercoaster I was experiencing for my loss was suddenly interrupted when a somewhat familiar man stood up to speak. As I watched him speak in memory of my dad, a realization took hold of me. I urgently asked the woman standing next to me if that man was who I thought he was. She confirmed that yes that was him. *That was Abuser A's son.* The memories of what happened at that dirty house came flooding back and the room spun as I struggled to breathe and stay calm, not wanting to cause a scene at my dad's funeral. I clutched my husband's arm, steadying myself, and told him who the speaker was. It was incredibly difficult to be around that man, even though he was not the one who abused me. In the moment, a part of me acknowledged that it was not this man's fault that his mere presence dredged up long-quiet memories about one of the most horrible encounters I had ever experienced. When this man walked up to me toward the end of the service, to give me his condolences personally, I froze. His words were muffled by my racing thoughts and pounding heart. Throughout the entire time interacting with him, I kept looking at my husband a few feet away. His presence kept me anchored, reminding me that I was a grown woman now, not a five-year-old little girl anymore.

When I first became a stepmother in the 90's, my stepdaughter was the same age that I was when Abuser B lived with my family. I was overly protective of her and often anxious when she stayed with us. At first, I was uncertain whether my feelings toward her were rooted in my natural urge to nurture and protect or if there was something more happening beneath the surface. Therapy helped me recognize that my behaviors and feelings about protecting my stepdaughter were in part a reaction to my own experiences at her age.[35] To release some of my anxiety, I decided to

---

[35] "Concern for the next generation is always linked to the question of prevention. The survivor's overriding fear is a repetition of the trauma; her goal is to prevent a repetition at all costs." Ibid., 206.

hire a private detective to locate Abuser B. I was aware the fifteen-year statute of limitation of assault had expired by this point, but that was not a deterrent. I just needed to know that he was not near me or my family. The detective was able to find Abuser B's general location, out of state. At that point, I froze.

Although the traumas I had experienced during my childhood and adolescence were years behind me, the effects continued to linger. Intrusive, unwelcome thoughts of my own death in the water were frequent. I have sat in a hot tub or a pool and could feel myself lying back, head starting to slip beneath the water's surface, tempted by the finality of death. I am still unable to sleep in a bed whose sheets are not perfectly clean. I always made sure that there was not a single piece of dirt I could feel, otherwise, I would not be able to sleep until it was taken care of. This hypervigilance was often distracting, preventing me from sitting down to relax if the dishes were not clean, or if I saw the need to dust or vacuum. I understand now that many of these behaviors were a way my mind tried to maintain control over a situation. I couldn't control what had happened to me, but I could keep my home clean and tidy. I continued to struggle with flurries of negative cognitions, beating myself up for not being good enough and blaming myself for things that were not my fault. My mind would jump to conclusions about the motivations of others, or I would get mad at others not doing what I thought they *should* be doing. This style of thinking was often the root of many arguments I had with my husband. Thankfully, therapy taught me that I had to make sure my expectations were clear, otherwise, I had no right to get upset. Learning how to communicate in a clear, assertive manner has helped empower me to say what I mean, and to know that I deserve to be heard.

Finding supportive people and using effective mental health practices have provided me with the skills of understanding the way my mind worked. For a long time, when I talked or thought about the abuse, I described it happening to 'the five-year-old little girl' or 'the eight-year-old little girl.' I had been trying so hard for so long to disconnect from the experiences and distance myself from them. I knew that this distancing was not working, avoiding the memories was not helping me, and that if I wanted to heal, I would have to confront them head-on. With support of my therapists, I was encouraged to talk to these little girls—to ask them what they could have done to prevent it or tell them what I thought they needed to hear to feel safe. After connecting to the little girl who had never really left me, I told her it was not her fault. That was the best part of therapy for me—acknowledging that the pain, wrong-doings, and abuse were not my fault. Once I was able to understand my powerlessness over what happened, I felt the truth of my blamelessness resonate within me. It wasn't just a platitude or something to say, it was reality. I began to untangle my confusion about my behaviors and faulty coping mechanisms. I learned that in order to survive; I did what I could with what little power I had.

24

BEING SEEN

"Folk wisdom recognizes that to forgive is divine. And even divine forgiveness, in most religious systems, is not unconditional. True forgiveness cannot be granted until the perpetrator has sought and earned it through confession, repentance, and restitution. Genuine contrition in a perpetrator is a rare miracle. Fortunately, the survivor does not need to wait for it. Her healing depends on the discovery of restorative love in her own life; it does not require that this love be extended to the perpetrator."[36]

When I became a young adult and started my own family, I asked my parents why I was not sent to therapy or why no legal consequences happened to my abusers. I loved them as much as any child could love their parents and knew that as much as I loved them, they loved me more. Even so, their ability to discuss such topics was not included in their otherwise strong parenting skill set. I found it unfortunate that the response my dad gave was that 'it happens to people and they get over it or just forget it.' Mom would ask rhetorically what else they could have done in a way that made me feel dismissed. It was not until I was forty-five years old that my dad and I talked again about what happened and about what *could* have been done to support me—then and now. This conversation was heartfelt, and dad seemed to genuinely listen to how I had felt for all those years. He validated my feelings and said that he had also been thinking about that

---

[36] Ibid., 190.

more recently, and he apologized to me. It was then that I realized that it wasn't an apology that I needed from my parents. I just needed them to know how I was feeling on the inside. I needed them to see me. I know that they would have never done anything to intentionally hurt me. The understanding I have of this supports the notion that they only wanted to ignore such things because they did not know how to make them go away.

My brothers had their own responses to my disclosure about being a survivor. My big brother was supportive as far as I can remember. I don't know what kind of relationship he had with Abuser B or for how long after, if at all. When I mentioned that I was writing a book about my trauma, I asked him some questions about the timeline about when Abuser B lived with us. I was disappointed when his response to my inquiries were summed up in two tiny words: "Oh, that." Although his response was not as informative as I was hoping for, I can guess that he, like so many others, felt it was best to let the past go. I can't blame him for that philosophy. I just wish it were that simple for me.

Growing up with my younger brother, we had a conflicted relationship. He often had less than sweet things to say about how he felt about me whenever I walked into the room. As an adult, I can see how his not so funny jokes were probably an attempt to cope with his own stuff. As a kid, a lot of those verbal jabs left emotional marks and certain 'jokes' were more hurtful than others. More often than I wanted, a comment from him led me to be upset or cry in my room, pissed off and hurt. Thankfully, we have both grown and have had the opportunity to spend time getting to know each other. He and I were able to talk honestly, and he listened with an open mind to a lot of things about my past he did not know. I cannot tell you how happy it made my heart to feel *seen* after all these years.

Not everyone's story is the same and not everyone's response to surviving abuse or assault is the same. Hearing this story may be painful for some, but I truly hope it is helpful for other survivors. If my book can help or allow another survivor to read a relatable story, I will be happy beyond words. Perhaps it will help someone feel less isolated by their trauma, inspire a victim to reconsider themselves as a survivor, or inform the reader on how to better protect and support the children they care for. My deepest hope for this book is that it inspires the reader to care for themselves and love who they are.

25

WRITING THIS BOOK

"Social action can take many forms, from concrete engagement with particular individuals to abstract intellectual pursuits. Survivors may focus their energies on helping others who have been similarly victimized, on educational, legal, or political efforts to prevent others from being victimized in the future, or on attempts to bring offenders to justice. Common to all these efforts is a dedication to raising public awareness. Survivors understand full well that the natural human response to horrible events is to put them out of mind. They may have done this themselves in the past. Survivors also understand that those who forget the past are condemned to repeat it. It is for this reason that public truth-telling is the common denominator of all social action."[37]

I am expecting critical feedback or even backlash for writing this book. I'm exposing my memories, releasing monsters, and breaking the social comfort zones of silence and avoidance. I can imagine the responses from others: *Why now? What are you trying to prove? Why haven't you reported this already? Why didn't you…?* I want to shout at these imaginary accusers in my defense, 'I would have! But…' Honestly, there are just so many reasons to not disclose sexual abuse, no matter what age you are when it happened, or how many years have passed.

---

[37] Ibid., 208.

Talking about trauma is difficult. It forces the victim to relive the traumatic event and it forces the audience to bear witness to humanity's capacity for evil. Witnessing trauma is never pleasant, and it is human nature to avoid uncomfortable situations.[38] I had learned by the reactions of my friends and family to previous disclosures that talking about what happened to me made people avoid the topic all together. When you already feel so alone, the thought of your nurturers and loved ones pushing you away for any reason is too painful to bear. By remaining silent, I protected everyone else; my parents, my attackers, and my community went on undisturbed.

My reasons for not disclosing what happened to me has evolved over the years. As a small child, I was fearful of being punished for doing something bad. I could not comprehend the traumatic experiences for what they were—an attack. How can one express what one cannot comprehend? As I grew, I began to understand more about the wrongness of what had happened and did not want to be judged by others for being involved in something so awful. Poor self-esteem as a teen led me to think that even if I could tell someone, they would not want to hear my story. Why would they care? After the trauma kept repeating in different situations with different abusers, I began to believe that it was pointless to try to seek justice. What was the point? Every time I had been sexually assaulted, the abusers would be shooed away, and I would be left to sort out my broken pieces.

Another reason that prevented me from disclosing at the time of the trauma was that the abusers were people my family and I knew. None of my abusers were strangers, lurking in the dark, waiting to pounce on random prey. They were neighbors, friends, trusted adults, and boyfriends. The abusers were strategic, relying on intimidation and the power imbalance between themselves and me to maintain their secrets.[39] By all means, continue to make safe choices about which alleys you chose to walk down

---

[38] "It is very tempting to take the side of the perpetrator. All the perpetrator asks is that the bystander do nothing. He appeals to the universal desire to see, hear, and speak no evil. The victim, on the contrary, asks the bystander to share the burden of pain. The victim demands action, engagement, and remembering." Ibid., 7-8.

[39] "In order to escape accountability for his crimes, the perpetrator does everything in his power to promote forgetting. Secrecy and silence are the perpetrator's first line of defense." Ibid., 8.

late at night. The message I am hoping to communicate is that the danger is most often closer and more familiar than we assume.

Despite all the reasons not to, I did attempt to share what happened to me before now. Unfortunately, those who have not personally experienced sexual abuse can unintentionally respond to disclosures in ways that are shaming or hurtful. I became very astute at recognizing the body language of someone who was unable to discuss the hard stuff that required them to be supportive. When this happened, I would just stop talking or change the subject to make them feel less uncomfortable. It seemed like I was just doing more damage if I brought it up. The feedback I got from people when they heard my story varied from uncomfortable silence to expressions of sincere empathy. I have had people cry with me and offer comfort while others gave advice. I had a close friend acknowledge that they had no idea how I felt but gave me the advice to 'leave the situation alone' as they had chosen to do with a different, unrelated situation in their own life. Sometimes people became defensive when they heard my story. Against what, I'm not sure.

These experiences with disclosure in part impacted my efforts to file an official report. I was unsure what the outcome would be and was terrified of being dismissed or worse, blamed, for what happened to me. I decided that it would be best to go somewhere that had support for people like me and then figure it out from there. The first time I drove to the Sexual Assault Support Services (SASS) to make a report, I turned around halfway there. I had an anxiety attack on the freeway and when the panic died down, all I wanted was to just go home. The next two times I went to SASS were about a year apart. I would complete a session about the process of reporting and then leave. The process of reporting felt daunting and there was no guarantee that I would receive any form of justice. I was hesitant to dig up all my worst memories just to be left alone and vulnerable again[40].

---

[40] "Efforts to seek justice or redress often involve further traumatization, for the legal system is often frankly hostile to rape victims. Even those who are well prepared are placed at a disadvantage by the systematic legal bias and institutional discrimination against them. The legal system is designed to protect men from the superior power of the state but not to protect women or children from the superior power of men. It therefore provides strong guarantees for the rights of the accused but essentially no guarantees for the rights of the victim." Ibid., 72.

Not long after I had attempted to make my second report at SASS, I watched alongside the world as the #MeToo movement gained serious momentum. Watching survivors come forward with their experiences and defying their abusers triggered a lot of emotions for me, as it did many, I'm sure. It was overwhelming at first. When I would hear something about the Nasser cases, I would cry for the survivors until I could barely breathe. I stopped watching the news for weeks. As the movement continued, I felt sick to my stomach about the growing number of confirmed sexual assault cases. There were so *many*. I felt guilty for not making my own reports by then. I thought about how different it was from forty years ago when it was 'good enough' to just strongly request that the abuser just not come around again. The movement inspired me to return to writing this book and follow through with making official reports. My journey is not yet complete, but I'm moving forward every day.

RESOURCES FOR SURVIVORS AND THEIR FAMILIES

Who can I ask for help?

The National Sexual Assault Hotline is available 24/7.
Telephone: (800) 656-HOPE (4673)
Online chat: online.rainn.org
Español: rainn.org/es

Calling the National Sexual Assault Hotline gives you access to a range of free services including:

- Confidential support from a trained staff member
- Support finding a local health facility that is trained to care for survivors of sexual assault and offers services like sexual assault forensic exams
- Someone to help you talk through what happened
- Local resources that can assist with your next steps toward healing and recovery
- Referrals for long term support in your area
- Information about the laws in your community
- Basic information about medical concerns

How can I help someone who has been sexually assaulted? What should I say?

Be patient as they open up. Listen to them. Believe them. Be supportive.

When someone has been sexually assaulted, they feel very vulnerable. They are often afraid they will not be believed or that they will be blamed for the assault. One of the best things you can do is acknowledge how difficult it was to say something and that you are honored they trusted you enough to talk about what was done to them.

Encourage them to seek help. Offer to be there for any of the things they might be going through, like going to the hospital or police.

Try saying:

- "I am so sorry this was done to you."
- "This was not your fault."
- "I'm honored you trust me and told me this."
- "What do you need the most right now? How can I help?"
- "Would you like me to take you to the hospital for an exam?" *(If the assault happened within the last 10 days.)*

There are also things you should *avoid* doing:

- Don't say "I can't believe that person would do such a thing." It implies you do not believe the sexual assault occurred.
- Do not ask for extra details the survivor does not provide themselves.
- Don't try to "fix it."
- Don't minimize it.
- Don't ask "why" questions. They are interpreted as blaming. Fear of being blamed is a huge part of why victims/survivors do not seek help.

How can I prevent my child from experiencing sexual abuse?

It is important to provide children with age-appropriate sex education as well as sexual abuse. Just as we teach our children about safety when crossing the street, it is important to teach them about sexual abuse. Children must be told in a matter-of-fact way that their bodies belong to *them* and that they have the right to say "no" to a "not-okay" touch. In addition, children and adolescents can be taught how to make safe decisions about where they go and what they do when there is no parental or adult supervision.

Teach your child that their body belongs to *them*. Emphasize that if they feel uncomfortable in the way they are being touched, they can tell the person "NO!" Explain that saying "NO!" can sometimes be difficult to do, especially if they are feeling scared, shy, or embarrassed. But the next thing they can do after saying "NO!" is to "GO"—get away from that person. Next, and the most important thing to do, is to "TELL"—although that can also be hard to do, it is very important to tell an adult they trust (e.g., their parent, other family member, coach, or teacher) about what happened. Teach your child that they must continue to tell what happened until someone listens and helps. Remember the steps: *NO-GO-TELL!*

It is important to remember that parents cannot watch and supervise their children all the time. Therefore, *no matter what you do, you may be unable to ensure that your child is never sexually abused.* As a nonabusive parent, you should not blame yourself if your child discloses sexual abuse. Instead, it is most helpful to use your energy to obtain any services your child may need.

A brief list of books about enhancing safety and body safety is included toward the end of this section.

How do I respond if I suspect my child has experienced sexual abuse?

The most important thing to do is *stay calm*. It is natural for parents to feel extremely distressed or angry upon discovering that their child may have been sexually abused. Children, including adolescents, are very sensitive to parental emotional reactions, and if they see or feel how upset or angry you are, that may cause them to "clam up" to prevent their parent from experiencing these emotions.

It is important to tell your child that it was good that they told you what happened. If you feel that you are unable to ask your child questions about the abuse calmly, it is best to wait for a professional's help.

Be careful to not say anything that sounds like you blame the child and emphasize that what happened was *not their fault*. It is *always* the adult's responsibility to set appropriate limits.

Where should I go for help for my child?

If you suspect that a child has been sexually abused, you should contact the child protection agency in their state/province. Most states have a 24-hour toll-free number for this purpose. You have the option to remain anonymous, but the caseworker will ask you important questions about the child, the possible offender, and the circumstances. The agency will most likely investigate the sexual abuse allegations and provide guidance on how to help the child and family.

Examples of books about sex education, enhancing safety, and body safety:

Annunziata, Jane, Denise Ortakales, and Maureen Tracy Patrolia. *Sex and Babies: First Facts*. Washington, D.C.: Magination Press, 2003.

Cole, Joanna. *Asking About Sex & Growing Up*. New York, NY: HarperCollins, 2009.

King, Zack, Kimberly King, Ramá Sue, and Sandra L. Caron. *I Said No!: a Kid-to-Kid Guide to Keeping Private Parts Private*. Weaverville, CA: Boulden Publishing, 2018.

Rosenzweig, Janet. *Sex-Wise Parent: the Parent's Guide to Talking to Children about Sex, Abuse, Bullying, And*. New York, NY: Skyhorse Publishing, 2012.

Sanders, Jayneen, and Sarah Jennings. *Let's Talk about Body Boundaries, Consent & Respect: a Book to Teach Children about Body Ownership, Respectful Relationships, Feelings and Emotions, Choices, and Recognizing Bullying Behaviors*. Macclesfield, Vic: Educate2Empower Publishing, an imprint of UpLoad Publishing, 2018.

ABOUT THE AUTHOR

Laura Chill is a life-time learner and has over thirty years' experience studying early childhood development and behaviors. After running her own childcare and preschool program, Laura completed a bachelor's degree in child development. After earning her degree, she went on to direct a larger childcare center for six years before her retirement from the childcare field.

Laura is grateful to have lived her life in the Pacific Northwest where she was born and raised. It was there that she raised her own two adult children to adulthood not far from her hometown. Laura claims Washington State as her home for forty-eight years and is now currently living in Western Oregon with her husband, dog, and two cats. When she is not working on her books, she is sketching, coloring, doing puzzles, playing drums, and presently re-learning calligraphy.

Currently she spends her time working in the mental health field, helping to support families and children who have experienced their own traumas.

BIBLIOGRAPHY

Chiba, Toshinori, Tetsufumi Kanazawa, Ai Koizumi, Kentarou Ide, Vincent Taschereau-Dumouchel, Shuken Boku, Akitoyo Hishimoto, et al. "Current Status of Neurofeedback for Post-Traumatic Stress Disorder: A Systematic Review and the Possibility of Decoded Neurofeedback." *Frontiers in Human Neuroscience* 13 (2019). https://doi.org/10.3389/fnhum.2019.00233.

Cohen, Judith A., Anthony P. Mannarino, and Esther Deblinger. *Treating Trauma and Traumatic Grief in Children and Adolescents*. Second Editioned. New York: The Guilford Press, 2017.

"Eye Movement Desensitization and Reprocessing (EMDR) Therapy." American Psychological Association. American Psychological Association. Accessed April 30, 2021. https://www.apa.org/ptsd-guideline/treatments/eye-movement-reprocessing.

Goldsmith, Rachel E., Christina Gamache Martin, and Carly Parnitzke Smith. "Systemic Trauma." *Journal of Trauma & Dissociation* 15, no. 2 (2014): 117–32. https://doi.org/10.1080/15299732.2014.871666.

Gurung, Kesherie. "Bodywork: Self-Harm, Trauma, and Embodied Expressions of Pain." *Arts and Humanities in Higher Education* 17, no. 1 (2018): 32–47. https://doi.org/10.1177/1474022216684634.

Herman, Judith Lewis. *Trauma and Recovery: the Aftermath of Violence-from Domestic Abuse to Political Terror*. New York, NY: Basic Books, 2015.

Kassem, Suzy, and Ryan Grim. *Rise up and Salute the Sun: the Writings of Suzy Kassem*. Boston, MA: Awakened Press, 2011.

Miller, Steven. "Twin Peaks Film Location – Centennial Log." Web log, September 15, 2018. https://www.twinpeaksblog.com/2018/09/15/twin-peaks-film-location-centennial-log/#more-6140.

Rauch, Sheila A., Afsoon Eftekhari, and Josef I. Ruzek. "Review of Exposure Therapy: A Gold Standard for PTSD Treatment." *The Journal of Rehabilitation Research and Development* 49, no. 5 (2012): 679–88. https://doi.org/10.1682/jrrd.2011.08.0152.

Summit, Roland C. "The Child Sexual Abuse Accomodation Syndrome." *Child Abuse & Neglect* 7, no. 2 (1983): 177–93. https://doi.org/10.1016/0145-2134(83)90070-4.

Van der Kolk, Bessel. *The Body Keeps the Score: Brain, Mind, and Body in the Healing of Trauma*. New York, NY: Penguin Books, 2015.

Printed in the United States
by Baker & Taylor Publisher Services